DRAWING
COMPLETE QUESTION & ANSWER
HANDBOOK

DRAWING
COMPLETE QUESTION & ANSWER
HANDBOOK
TRUDY FRIEND

D&C
David and Charles

In memory of Kara

A DAVID & CHARLES BOOK

Copyright © David & Charles Limited 2011

David & Charles is an imprint of F&W Media International, LTD

Brunel House, Forde Close, Newton Abbot, TQ12 4PU, UK

F&W Media International, LTD is a subsidiary of F+W Media, Inc., 4700 East Galbraith Road

Cincinnati OH45236, USA

First published in the UK in 2011

First published in the US in 2011

Copyright @ Trudy Friend 2011

ISBN-13: 978-0-7153-3834-6

ISBN-10: 0-7153-3834-X

10 9 8 7 6 5 4 3 2 1

Printed in China RR Donnelley for:

F&W Media International, LTD

Brunel House, Forde Close, Newton Abbot, TQ12 4PU, UK

F+W Media publishes high quality books on a wide range of subjects

Website: www.rubooks

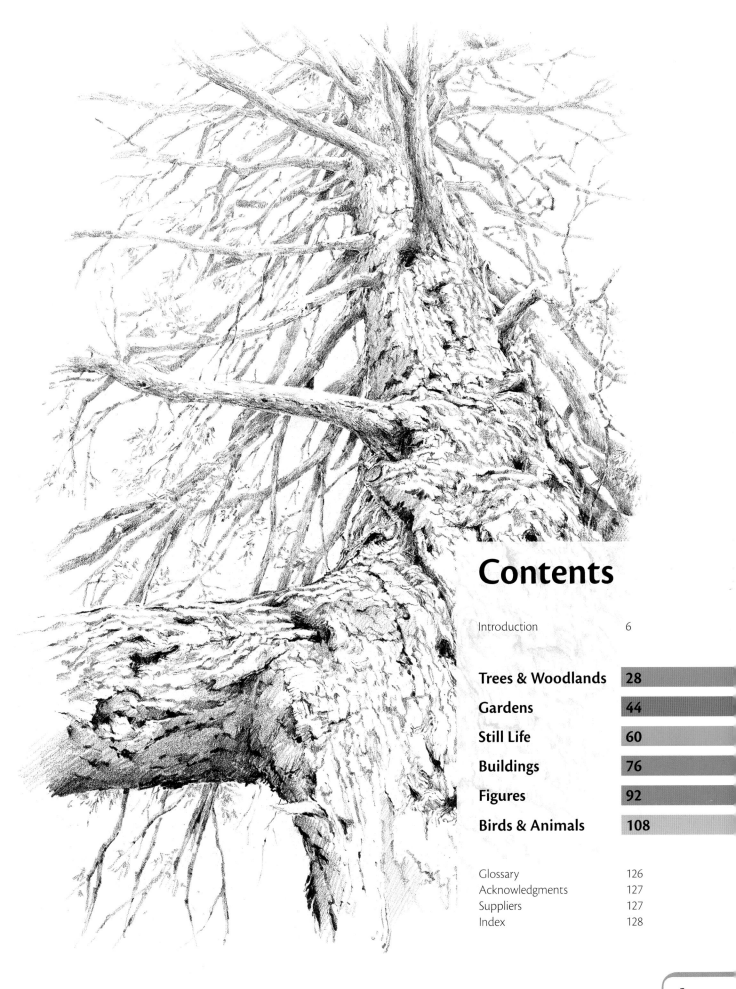

Contents

Introduction

With this book I will be helping you
To love your art
To live your art
And see the world go by
As tone and texture, line and form
And with an artist's eye

From an early age we learn by asking questions and reacting to the answers received from other people. We can learn to draw in the same way, by asking questions of ourselves as well as others. The aim of this book is to offer direct, practical solutions to the most common questions on drawing approach and technique that constantly arise as we learn to draw and expand on our skills.
The book is divided into six sections, covering a wide range of subject matter: trees and woodlands, gardens, still life, buildings, figures, and birds and animals. The focus is on graphite drawing throughout, which is an excellent starting point for all your artwork and will help you to master brushstrokes (see page 125) as well as other drawing materials. Working in monochrome encourages consideration for tonal values and use of strong contrasts that will add drama to your interpretations. I hope the questions I have chosen as headings to the following pages along with the answers, given in the form of illustrations and technique suggestions, are of help to you with the development of your own drawing methods.

This lily study was executed with a smooth on/off pressure stroke – see page 18.

A preliminary drawing, such as this quick figure sketch, examines some of the questions that the artist would have to consider in order to achieve a convincing detailed representation of the final work.

Mark Making

Representational drawing involves making marks (used individually or combined) that effectively create impressions of the subjects you choose to depict. Examples of marks for you to practise are demonstrated on pages 10–11.

On pages 18–21 you will see how a series of marks based on just eight simple pencil stroke applications can be used in various combinations for the depiction of any subject matter.

Developing Observational Skills

In order to make our drawn images recognizable we need to develop observational skills by looking closely at our subjects and trying to understand as much about them as possible before embarking on an investigative sketch. Preliminary sketches are important if we wish to represent subjects convincingly.

Ask yourself the question: 'does my representation look believable?' And, if not, 'why?' I hope that you will find the answers to your questions within the themes of this book.

Here, I have used guidelines to position the stones, to establish their correct proportions and relationships with interesting 'shapes between'. The sheep were added to enhance the composition.

Achieving Accuracy

Using a personal grid comprised of vertical and horizontal guidelines, drawn both over your reference material and on your first sketch (see page 58) rather than a rigid grid, will help you to line up corresponding shapes accurately.

These guidelines need only be of a length required to work effectively from one point to another to avoid confusion, and I will explain how to look for suitable 'V' shapes from which (and through which) to draw them.

Pictorial Composition

Controlling the way in which your drawings are viewed is important, by guiding the viewer's eye into your picture. This may be achieved in various ways, including consideration of format (shape of mount aperture), as explained on pages 38–39 and 44–45.

Perspective (see pages 56–57) and contrasts of tone, texture and shape, all need to be taken into consideration and you will find reference to these aspects throughout the book.

Asking Questions

Should you feel a drawing lacks drama or definition, ask yourself: 'why?' It may be that you are not making full use of the tonal values, by contrasting rich darks against areas of untouched (white) paper.

You may feel that perspective angles you have drawn appear incorrect and, if so, you can look at the problem in a different way, by drawing negative shapes between the objects in order to place them correctly. Often our answers rely on simple logic that may be arrived at just by asking questions of ourselves.

When you are drawing, just look at the simple tonal shapes. Forget the subject while you relate the shapes to each other within your composition (see page 88).

Forget the Subject

Preliminary (investigative) sketches are a good way to start drawings, giving opportunities to ask questions, for example: 'what else appears to be on the same level as a particular component?' You can then draw a guideline from a 'V' shape (see page 58) to answer your question, and in this way build the basis for your drawing.

At this early stage it is a good idea to try to forget the particular subject(s) you are drawing and concentrate on shapes and their relationships with each other. When this preliminary sketch is complete you can 'trace off' the essential lines on to quality paper and start the final artwork.

Q What graphite media are available to draw with?

A Here I have used a range from Derwent to explain a few examples.

TIP *Get to know your pencils by practising a variety of marks. Use various pressures for application and different paper surfaces to notice the effects*

Graphite Media

1. Graphic Pencils

These are high-quality pencils. They are very versatile and available in 20 degrees: from a soft, easy-to-blend 9B, from which you can produce dramatic, interesting sketches with strong contrasts of line and tone, to a crisp 9H. The harder grades lend themselves to fine line drawing and soft, subtle tonal interpretations.

2. Graphite Sticks

These are pure artist-quality graphite in the form of a solid stick and the water-soluble sticks may be used wet or dry. The Derwent range has four available strengths: 2B, 4B, 6B and 8B.

3. Natural Graphite Blocks

These are available in soft, medium and hard grades and their use encourages free interpretations. Alternating wide and sharp sides of the blocks will allow free, expressive graphite drawings to develop. Using the wide edge produces interesting textural effects.

4. Sketching and Water-Soluble Sketching Pencils

With their soft, extra-wide graphite strip, these are ideal for loose sketching and strong linear interpretations. They are available in three degrees as sketching pencils: HB, 2B and 4B. The water-soluble version is available in: HB, 4B and 8B.

Mark Making with Graphite Media

The following marks demonstrate the variety of effects that can be achieved by experimenting with a range of grades and types of graphite media.

Derwent Graphic: 9B

Derwent Graphic: H

Graphite stick: 8B

Graphite stick: 2B

Natural graphite block: soft

Natural graphite block: medium

Sketching and water-soluble sketching pencils: dark wash 8B

Water-soluble sketching pencil: medium wash 4B

Pencil Stroke Movements

With so many graphite tools available – blocks, sticks and pencils of various grades – mark making is a limitless experience. Here are just a few examples for you to practise in preparation for interesting image depiction.

1. Tonal block

9B pencil

Dot

Put or press

Dash

Directional line

Varied pressure line

2. Varied direction zigzag movement that crosses over other lines

Light pressure

Firm pressure

Varied pressure wandering line movement

3.

Dots massed: stippling

Dashes massed

Combination of dashes and dots massed

Combination of zigzag movement, dots and dashes

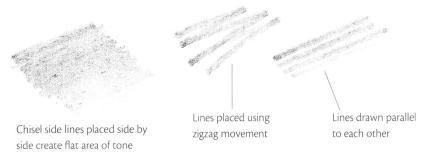

4. Tonal block to establish chisel side of pencil strip

Chisel side lines placed side by side create flat area of tone

Lines placed using zigzag movement

Lines drawn parallel to each other

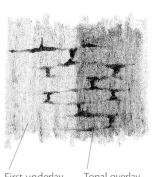

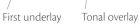

5. Applied vertically, using either method, a flat tonal area produces tone over which drawings may be superimposed

First underlay   Tonal overlay

On/off pressure lines create interest for the linear overdrawing

6. Smooth, flowing movements produce smooth, flowing marks

Unevenly applied pressure creates a textured effect useful for depicting a variety of subjects

Q What are the need-to-know marks for starting to draw?

 A Start by practising line and tone. Below and opposite are a number of applications for achieving a variety of pencil effects.

Line

There are three main types of lines that are useful in drawing:

1. Diagrammatic or 'wire-like' line

2. Erratic application line

3. On/off pressure line

Tone

To create tone, start by moving the pencil on the paper using firm pressure (a), then gradate into a paler tone by putting less pressure on the pencil as it moves across the paper (b).

a) Create dark tone with firm pressure of the pencil on the paper

b) Gradating into paler tone

TECHNIQUES: Line and Tone

Constant contact

Individually placed lines

Constant contact application of tone

Overlaying tones

Overlaying lines

Wide lines into narrow lines achieved by turning the pencil

Wide lines into narrow lines achieved by lifting and re-applying pressure on the pencil

Interesting lines created by twisting or rocking the pencil as it travels

Gradated Tonal Values in the Form of a Ribbon

Tonal ribbons are useful tools for practising achieving gradated light and dark tones with the pencil and for understanding the level of pressure needed on the pencil to achieve your desired tone.

Creating a Tonal Ribbon

Start with firm pressure of up and down strokes

Keep the strokes parallel to each other and touching (or overlapping) when forming solid tonal areas and vary the direction of application when creating your tonal ribbon

Creating a Sweeping Stroke

Sweeping strokes can be formed using the wide chisel side of the pencil. They are particularly useful for shadows within folds of cloth.

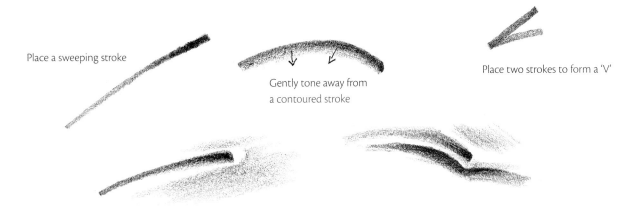

Place a sweeping stroke

Gently tone away from a contoured stroke

Place two strokes to form a 'V'

Using Sweeping Strokes when Studying Folds in Cloth

Practising shapes such as the ones below will help you to improve your representations of cloth.

Look for 'V' shapes and enhance with rich dark tone

Dark shadow recess shape

Untouched white paper represents lightest lights

Toning away from light edge

Q **Can you show me a typical range of pencil stroke movements to practise and explain how they may be achieved?**

A The following pencil stroke movements were made using a soft grade of drawing pencil (see grades from a typical range explained on page 28).

1. On/Off Pressure Stroke

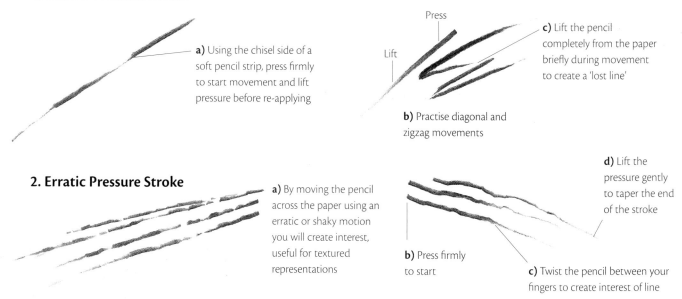

a) Using the chisel side of a soft pencil strip, press firmly to start movement and lift pressure before re-applying

Press

Lift

c) Lift the pencil completely from the paper briefly during movement to create a 'lost line'

b) Practise diagonal and zigzag movements

2. Erratic Pressure Stroke

a) By moving the pencil across the paper using an erratic or shaky motion you will create interest, useful for textured representations

d) Lift the pressure gently to taper the end of the stroke

b) Press firmly to start

c) Twist the pencil between your fingers to create interest of line

3. Zigzag Movement

a) Firm, even pressure, zigzag movement of the hand

b) Firm pressure

c) Light pressure, or lift from the paper completely

4. Grazing

Diagonal grazing of the pencil over the paper (in any direction) can be overlaid to increase intensity

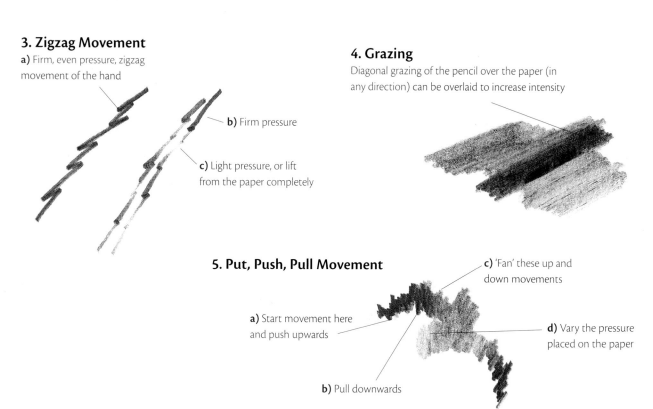

5. Put, Push, Pull Movement

c) 'Fan' these up and down movements

a) Start movement here and push upwards

d) Vary the pressure placed on the paper

b) Pull downwards

TIP *Make sure you create a chisel side to your pencil strip so that you can use this, and the resulting fine side, alternately*

6. Delicate Marks

By using only the very tip of a sharp point on your pencil you will be able to achieve delicate lines, zigzags, dots, etc.

7. Fanned Stroke Movement

A combination of short (massed) 'fanned' stroke movements of varied pressure, making use of untouched paper 'shapes between'

8. Working with a Light Form

a) Starting away from the light image that is to be depicted, work with uneven movements back towards the edge of the light form

b) This will create a dark background behind a light form

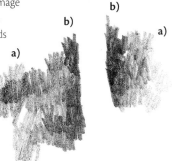

9. Sweeping Strokes

a) Start with a downward movement followed by a swift upward stroke: this is a continuous movement

b) Massing the resulting strokes from these movements (in different directions) creates an interesting variety of shapes

10. Contoured Strokes

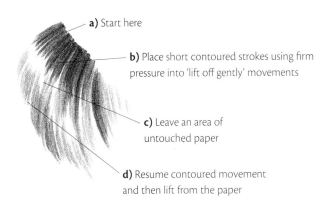

a) Start here

b) Place short contoured strokes using firm pressure into 'lift off gently' movements

c) Leave an area of untouched paper

d) Resume contoured movement and then lift from the paper

11. Variety

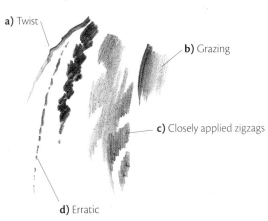

a) Twist

b) Grazing

c) Closely applied zigzags

d) Erratic

Q Can you demonstrate two totally different subjects that require similar stroke movements?

A The comb of this chicken received similar treatment to the rusty chain on the opposite page. Both subjects demonstrate the overlaying technique, using the grazing application (see page 19). The use of an unevenly (erratically) applied edge line to define shapes also adds interest to both studies.

Chicken Study

Cutting in: Using a sharp pencil, cut in with a dark tone behind a light form

Erratic movement: Vary the pressure on the pencil point as you define the edge of the form

MEDIA
- Derwent Graphic: 6B
- Copier paper

Stippling: Move the tip of the pencil down onto the paper's surface and swiftly lift and reapply. Massed, or separately applied marks achieve the effect of dark or light toned texture, depending on how close together they are placed

Sweeping strokes: Whether contoured or straight movements are used, these parallel strokes can be useful when describing form

Lost and found: It is not necessary to draw completely around any form. By losing some of the edges the image appears more accurately represented as we naturally see it

Overlaying: Build layers of darker line or tone over the initial pale tonal underdrawing

Edge lines: In order to avoid uninteresting diagrammatic outlines, vary the pressure you place on your pencil to create an interesting edge line

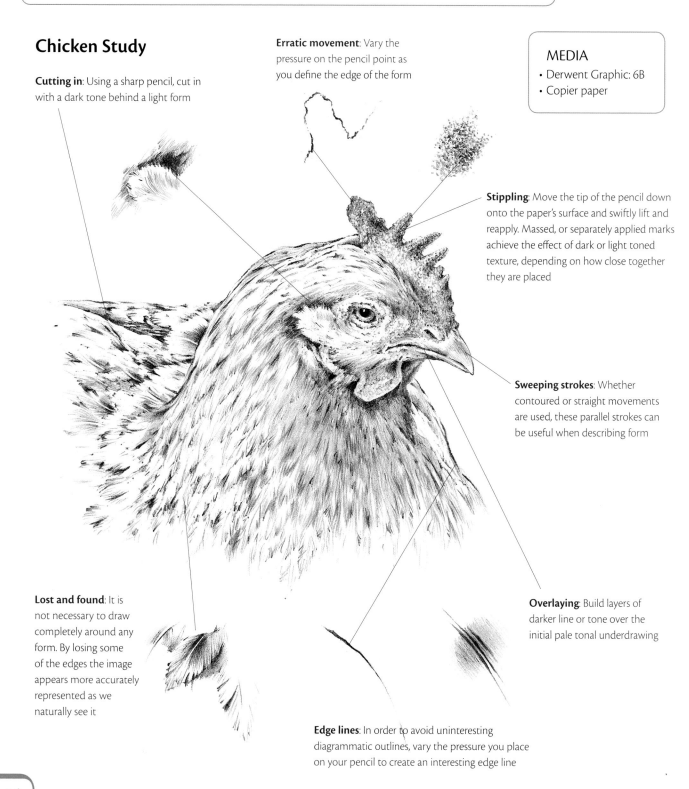

Chain Study

Tonal shapes: These may be drawn first and shadow shapes and lines overlaid

Negative shapes: These dark (shadow recess) shapes between stones and pebbles vary from narrow (erratically drawn) shapes to fine on/off pressure lines

Contoured texture: Short, varied direction 'push outwards and mass' stroke movements are similar to the stippling on the hen's comb opposite and they build textured tone to describe form

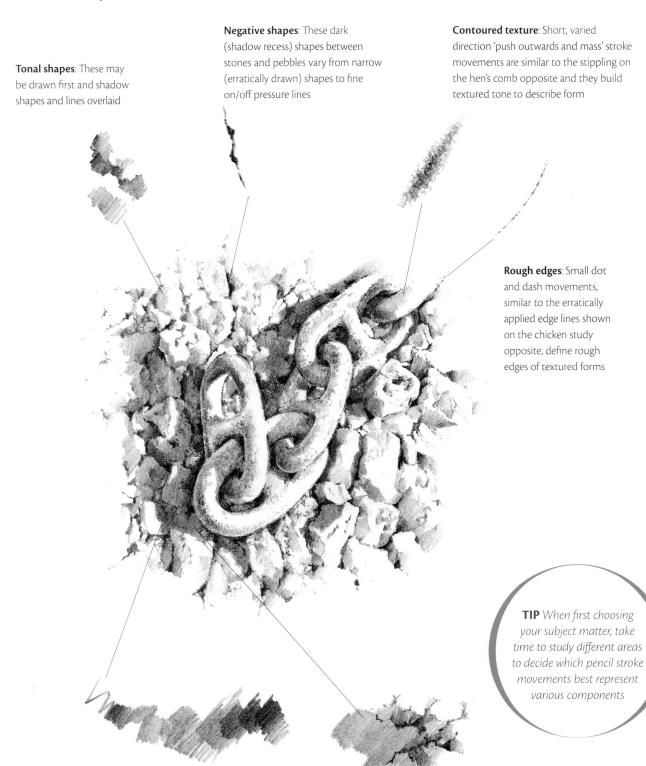

Rough edges: Small dot and dash movements, similar to the erratically applied edge lines shown on the chicken study opposite, define rough edges of textured forms

TIP *When first choosing your subject matter, take time to study different areas to decide which pencil stroke movements best represent various components*

Contrasts: Be aware of the tonal values and the importance of placing the darkest darks against the lightest lights for maximum drama and effect

Line and tone: Line and tone in cast shadow areas may either be applied alternately as you work, or as lines over tonal underlay or tone over a line drawing

The Eight Basic Strokes

Analysing the strokes I use in my own artwork, I have compiled a list of eight basic stroke applications that may be adapted in various ways for all subjects and textures and used in all pencil, ink and water-based media.

1. The On/Off Pressure Stroke

Smoothly applied, using a soft pencil, this movement creates interesting fluid shapes that can give an instant water ripple effect. Elongated versions are also useful for depicting areas of plants.

> **MEDIA**
> • Koh-I-Noor
>   Progresso: 6B
> • Copier paper

How to Execute the On/Off Pressure Stroke

When a soft pencil is used, it is easier to achieve width of stroke. Place pressure on the pencil during the movement and add a tapering end to the stroke as you lift the pencil from the paper.

Creating a Ripple Effect

Twist the pencil as you complete the stroke to taper the end. Use a number of on/off pressure strokes together to form a ripple effect.

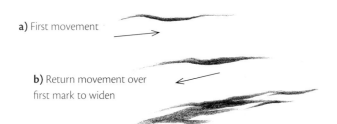

a) First movement

b) Return movement over first mark to widen

c) Backwards and forwards movements, overlapping and widening certain areas, will achieve the impression of water ripples

2. The Erratic Pressure Stroke

This stroke is very similar to the on/off pressure stroke above, but differs in that it is applied with erratic, or uneven, pressure on the pencil. Erratic pencil movements are useful for achieving texture on a variety of surfaces, as demonstrated here in relation to rocks and stones.

> **MEDIA**
> • Faber-Castell: 8B
> • Copier paper

How to Execute the Erratic Pressure Stroke

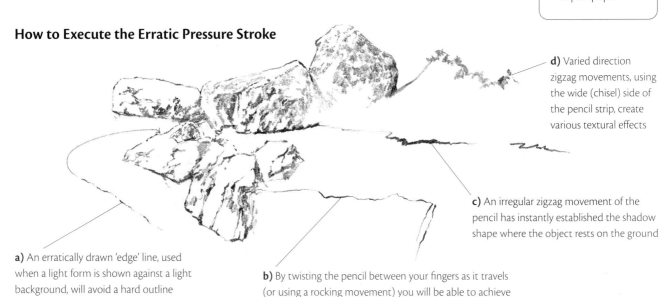

d) Varied direction zigzag movements, using the wide (chisel) side of the pencil strip, create various textural effects

c) An irregular zigzag movement of the pencil has instantly established the shadow shape where the object rests on the ground

a) An erratically drawn 'edge' line, used when a light form is shown against a light background, will avoid a hard outline

b) By twisting the pencil between your fingers as it travels (or using a rocking movement) you will be able to achieve an interesting line that depicts slim shadow recess shapes

3. The Grazing Application

Executed with a well-established chisel side to the pencil strip, a grazing application of wide strokes placed directionally against each other forms areas of tonal values that combine to create interesting contrasts against the white paper. This stroke provides smooth toning to indicate flat or contoured surfaces. The strokes may comprise parallel lines fusing together or crosshatch application, working through all the tonal values.

How to Execute the Grazing Application

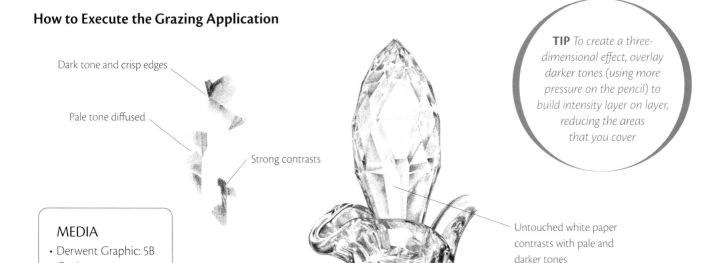

Dark tone and crisp edges

Pale tone diffused

Strong contrasts

TIP *To create a three-dimensional effect, overlay darker tones (using more pressure on the pencil) to build intensity layer on layer, reducing the areas that you cover*

Untouched white paper contrasts with pale and darker tones

MEDIA
- Derwent Graphic: 5B
- Copier paper

4. The Put, Push, Pull Application

The combination of push and pull that defines this application lends itself naturally to the depiction of foliage masses.

MEDIA
- Koh-I-Noor: 8B (soft grade pencil for maximum width of stroke)
- Copier paper

How to Execute the Put, Push, Pull Application

Foliage Mass

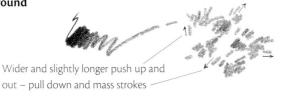

Short push up and pull down to create massed strokes

Ideal for foliage effects

Stony Ground

Wider and slightly longer push up and out – pull down and mass strokes

With more retention of untouched paper, stony ground may be represented

Flat Surfaces

Vertically massed push up and vertically massed pull down

These stroke movements offer instant tonal texture for flat surfaces

5. The 'On Your Toes' Application

In order to achieve delicate detail, use the very tip of your (sharpened) pencil, held vertical to the paper's surface, for any stroke movement.

MEDIA
• Derwent Graphic: B
• Copier paper

How to Execute the 'On Your Toes' Application

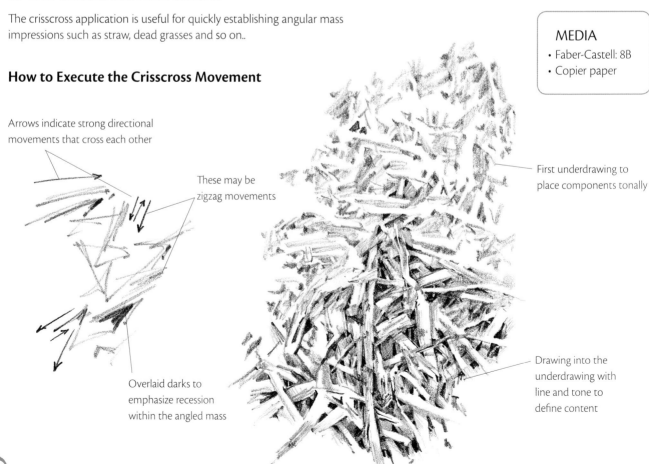

Erratically drawn texture lines indicate shadow recess in the texture of a dog's nose

Erratically drawn lines create texture

Fill in dark areas by delicately overlaying tonal application within untouched paper areas

Delicate swift contoured pull down strokes indicate shadow recess shapes between clumps of hair

Erratic application defines the edge of the nose originally, avoiding a hard, wire-like outline

Pull down strokes give the impression of light hairs in front of dark

6. The Crisscross Movement

The crisscross application is useful for quickly establishing angular mass impressions such as straw, dead grasses and so on..

MEDIA
• Faber-Castell: 8B
• Copier paper

How to Execute the Crisscross Movement

Arrows indicate strong directional movements that cross each other

These may be zigzag movements

First underdrawing to place components tonally

Overlaid darks to emphasize recession within the angled mass

Drawing into the underdrawing with line and tone to define content

7. The 'Up to and Away' Movement

When you are defining the edges of forms that are lighter in tone than the background area, it is important to avoid any background toning overlapping. 'Up to and away' provides an effective way of preventing this from happening. This is particularly useful when establishing backgrounds against light forms.

MEDIA
• Derwent Graphic: 4B
• Copier paper

How to Execute the 'Up to and Away' Movement

c) If you need to draw an 'edge' line as a guide, endeavour to absorb this line into the tone, to avoid outlines

b) When you have crisply clarified the light edge of image, move away into a dark negative shape or fade out to suggest a diffused tonal background

a) Apply tone by moving the chisel side of the pencil strip gently, in sideways movements, up to the edge of the light image

8. The Tick and Flick Movement

This useful stroke, when applied en masse is useful for creating highlights on hair, rope, flower petals and so on, as well as the strokes that instantly represent grasses.

TIP *If you are using a soft grade pencil remember to keep turning the pencil as you work and to sharpen it frequently*

How to Execute the Tick and Flick Movement

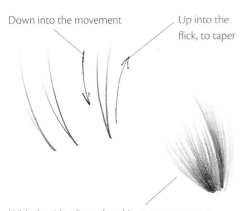

Down into the movement

Up into the flick, to taper

MEDIA
• Derwent Graphic: B
• Copier paper

With the side of your hand in constant contact with the surface of the paper, just move your thumb and the fingers that are holding the pencil. This is a downward movement that, on reaching the base of the stroke, immediately travels upwards into a flick that tapers as you lift from the paper

Repeat the movement to form a tonal mass that is contoured, you can represent a variety of textures, including that of hair, grasses and the effect of flower petals

Other Drawing Media

As this book concentrates on graphite drawing I will not mention the numerous coloured pencil ranges that are available, except to say that the stroke movements I have demonstrated on pages 18–21 for graphite interpretations are exactly the same as those I apply to all dry and water-soluble media. However, Derwent have a range of tinted drawing pencils (demonstrated on this page) and Graphitint, which is an exciting range of lightly tinted water-soluble graphite pencils (see page 123), that you might like to try with your graphite drawing techniques.

Derwent Drawing Pencils

This range of tinted drawing pencils is ideal for life and nature studies. Here, I have redrawn the eight basic stroke movements from pages 18–21 to demonstrate a few of the hues available. Below, I have also coloured part of an existing graphite study to demonstrate how a monochrome interpretation can be transformed by overlaying colour from these pencils.

The Eight Basic Stoke Movements in Subtle Hues

1. Ink Blue – On/off pressure movement

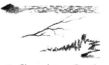

2. Chocolate – Erratic pencil movements

3. Warm Earth – Grazing movement into blending

4. Olive Earth – Put, push, pull movements

5. Venetian Red – 'On your toes' for delicate cutting in and texture

6. Crag Green – Crisscross movement

7. Sepia (Red) – 'Up to and away' – to bring a light form forward

8. Sanguine – Tick and flick – useful for grass and hair interpretations

Adding Colour to a Graphite Drawing

MEDIA
• Derwent Graphic: 4B (original drawing)
• Derwent Drawing (colour over drawing)
• Bristol board

These soft drawing pencils have a unique creamy texture and provide a colour range that includes greens, blues and greys

The rich velvety finish of these colours means they mix beautifully when burnished on top of each other. When blended over graphite drawing they combine to create subtle hue and tone

Charcoal

Charcoal was one of the earliest drawing materials ever used, and is still a versatile and popular medium.

Using Tinted Charcoal

Derwent charcoal pencils are available in three grades: light, medium and dark, providing a wide tonal range

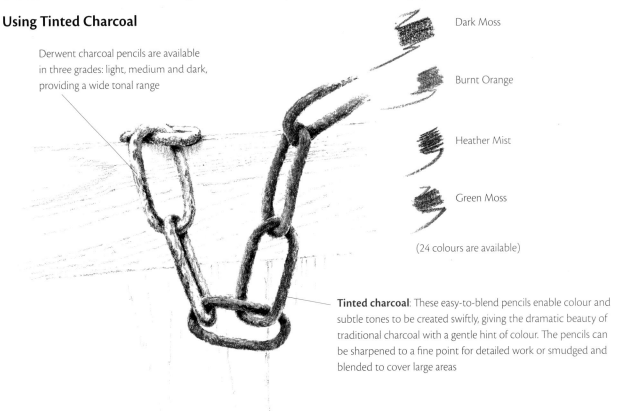

Dark Moss

Burnt Orange

Heather Mist

Green Moss

(24 colours are available)

Tinted charcoal: These easy-to-blend pencils enable colour and subtle tones to be created swiftly, giving the dramatic beauty of traditional charcoal with a gentle hint of colour. The pencils can be sharpened to a fine point for detailed work or smudged and blended to cover large areas

Forms of Charcoal

Compressed charcoal is a round block of pure reformed wood charcoal. Both charcoal pencils and compressed charcoal are available in light, medium and dark.

1. Charcoal Pencil

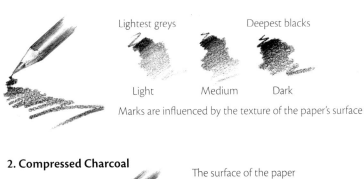

Lightest greys

Deepest blacks

Light   Medium   Dark

Marks are influenced by the texture of the paper's surface

2. Compressed Charcoal

The surface of the paper will determine the textured effect created

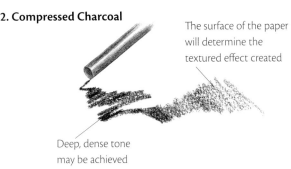

Deep, dense tone may be achieved

Charcoal Pencil Sketchbook Studies: Dog

These loose studies of a Basset Hound show the effects that can be achieved with charcoal.

Q Can you suggest how I could work indoors using an object as reference that will help me understand more about depicting a different subject seen outdoors?

 A There are many objects we can draw when working indoors where techniques used in their execution relate to those used for the depiction of outdoor subjects. For example, the cases of the cupcakes shown on pages 64–65 will help you understand how to draw corrugated iron on a building. Drawing a vegetable such as a parsnip (see below) provides excellent reference material for the depiction of tree roots and similar forms.

Indoor Parsnip Study

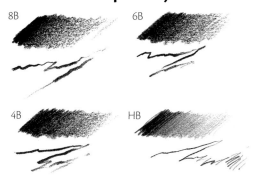

8B   6B

4B   HB

Test your grades on the paper's surface before deciding which one to use for your drawing

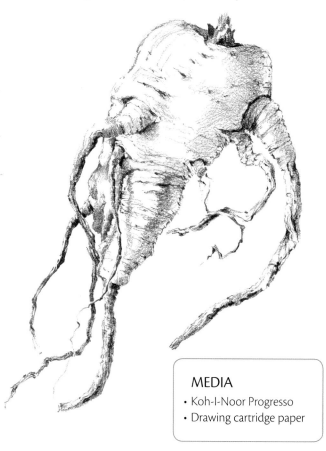

MEDIA
• Koh-I-Noor Progresso
• Drawing cartridge paper

TECHNIQUES

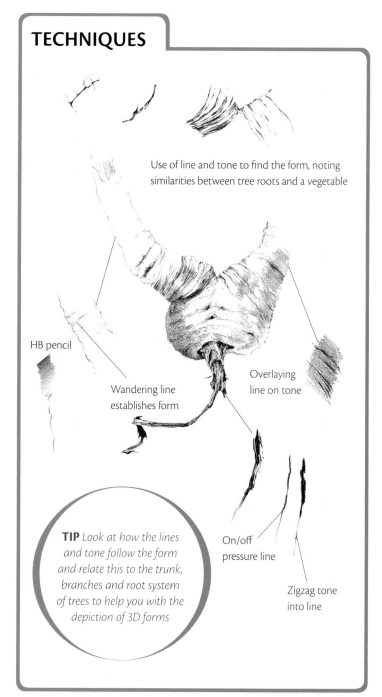

Use of line and tone to find the form, noting similarities between tree roots and a vegetable

HB pencil

Wandering line establishes form

Overlaying line on tone

On/off pressure line

Zigzag tone into line

TIP Look at how the lines and tone follow the form and relate this to the trunk, branches and root system of trees to help you with the depiction of 3D forms

Outdoor Tree Study

Quick diagonal strokes suggest a stronger tone in the background area, seen at a distance

This 'busy' area of rough bark, ivy leaves and twigs contrasts with the relatively smooth texture of the trunk in front

MEDIA
• Derwent Graphic soft pencil
• Copier paper

Counterchange – light form in front of dark background and dark in front of a lighter tone

I have enlarged my sketch of the tree root area (in relation to the rest of the study) in order to emphasize the similarities between this and the parsnip study opposite

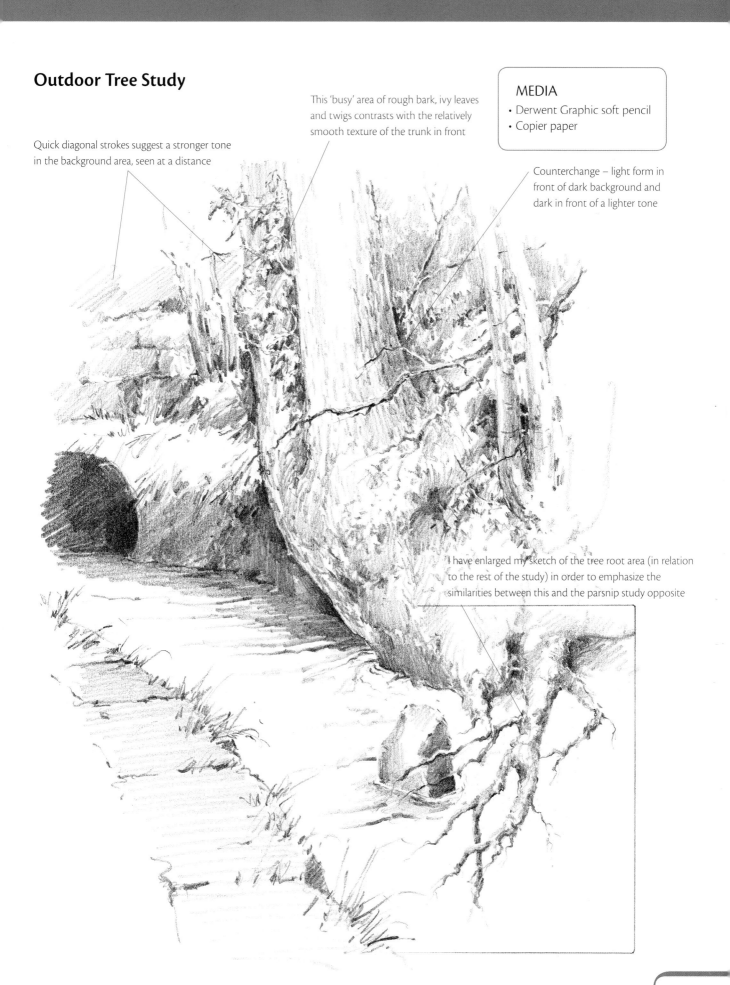

25

Can the guideline method of achieving accuracy be used to help with the depiction of many different subjects? Can you show one or two examples and demonstrate the use of perspective lines in relation to a simple object?

A Guidelines, in the form of a personal grid, can help you to achieve an accurate drawing for any subject, by relating components to each other.

Dog Study

Use guidelines and 'shapes between' in the investigative stages in order to make any necessary alterations, before progressing to create an accurate study.

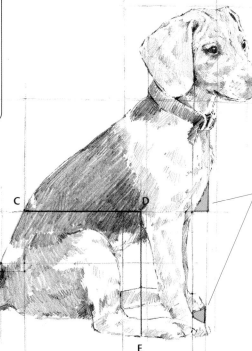

1. Distance: Note that A to B, C to D and D to E all measure the same distance

2. 'Shapes between': The use of an external guideline like this will give you abstract shapes to help achieve the correct angles

Horse and Carriage

Compare the simple side view of the dog, above, with the more complex relationship of the horse and carriage in this illustration.

These horizontal guidelines help relate the horse to the carriage

'Shapes between' parts of the carriage and external guidelines are helpful in positioning components

A drop line from the horse's shoulder helps to position this leg back, under the body weight slightly

House Study

This is one of the preliminary sketches for the study on page 83 and demonstrates how guidelines help in relation to the representation of a building.

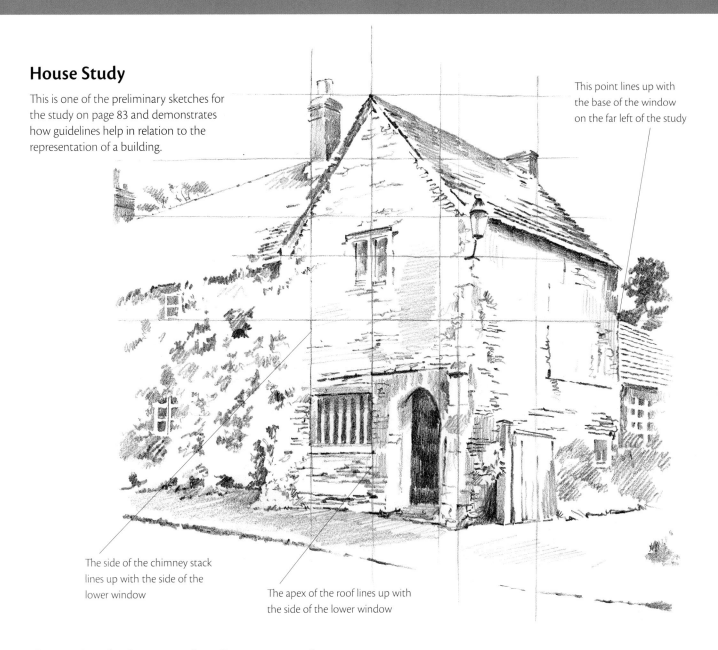

This point lines up with the base of the window on the far left of the study

The side of the chimney stack lines up with the side of the lower window

The apex of the roof lines up with the side of the lower window

Open Book: Perspective Demonstration

A simple object, such as an open book, requires consideration for perspective in the same way as for that of buildings and other subjects.

Perspective Lines

Vanishing point

Eye level

TREES & WOODLANDS

Trunk with Ivy

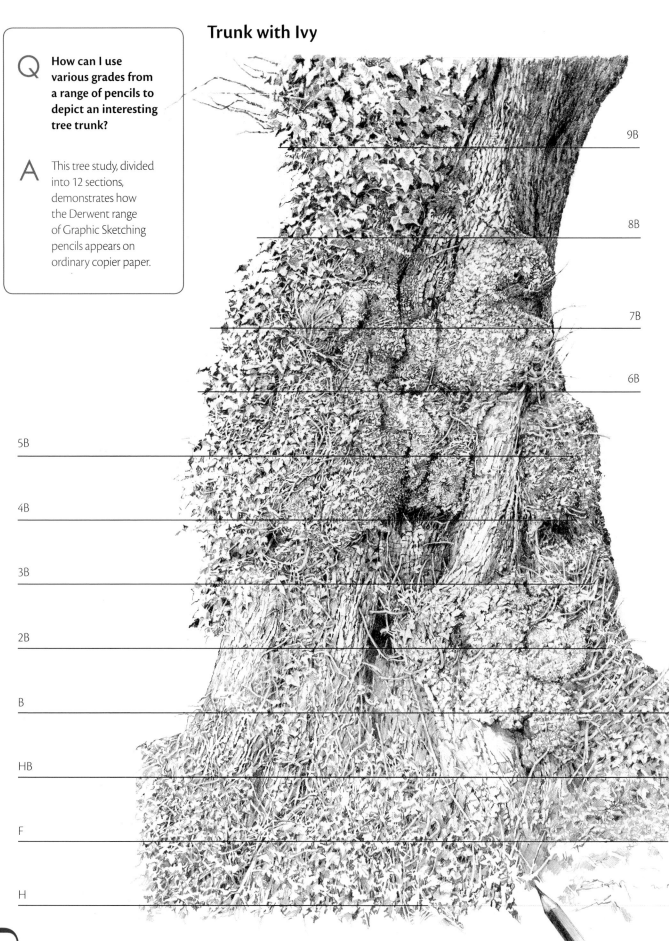

9B

8B

7B

6B

5B

4B

3B

2B

B

HB

F

H

Experimenting with Pencil Grades

Four grades taken from this range are demonstrated here to help you to understand some of the differences that can be experienced when using these pencils.

MEDIA
- Derwent Graphic Sketching: 9B, 5B, 2B, HB
- Copier paper

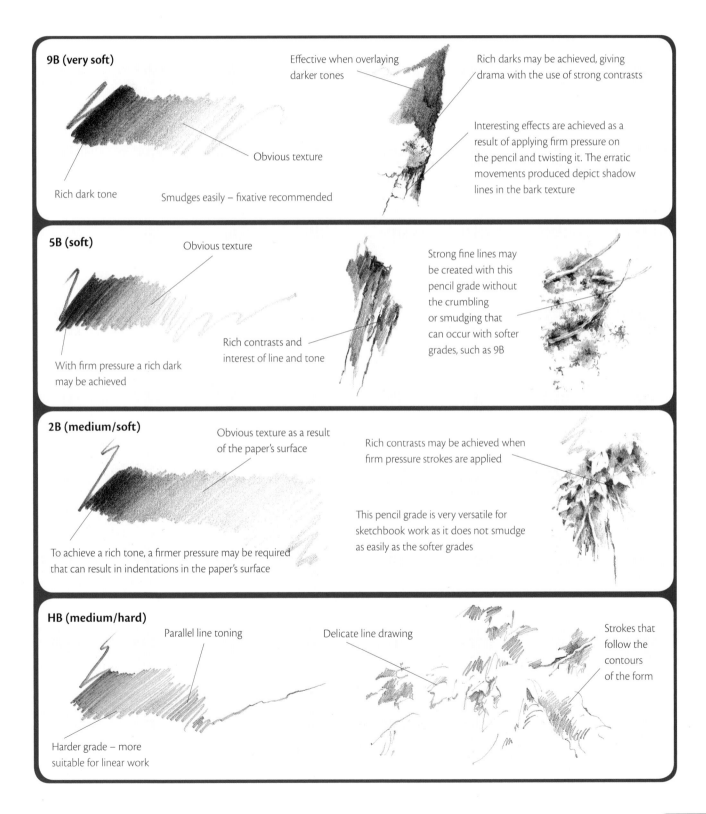

9B (very soft)

Effective when overlaying darker tones

Rich darks may be achieved, giving drama with the use of strong contrasts

Obvious texture

Interesting effects are achieved as a result of applying firm pressure on the pencil and twisting it. The erratic movements produced depict shadow lines in the bark texture

Rich dark tone

Smudges easily – fixative recommended

5B (soft)

Obvious texture

Strong fine lines may be created with this pencil grade without the crumbling or smudging that can occur with softer grades, such as 9B

With firm pressure a rich dark may be achieved

Rich contrasts and interest of line and tone

2B (medium/soft)

Obvious texture as a result of the paper's surface

Rich contrasts may be achieved when firm pressure strokes are applied

This pencil grade is very versatile for sketchbook work as it does not smudge as easily as the softer grades

To achieve a rich tone, a firmer pressure may be required that can result in indentations in the paper's surface

HB (medium/hard)

Parallel line toning

Delicate line drawing

Strokes that follow the contours of the form

Harder grade – more suitable for linear work

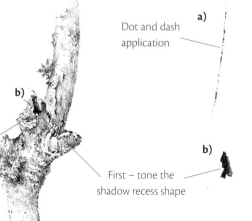

Q **How can I achieve bark texture effect and detail on twigs?**

A Practise the line and tone exercises demonstrated below:

Studying Bark Texture

Find a small piece of bark and study the tonal lines and shapes. Start at the top and work downwards, just drawing what you see and remembering to leave areas of untouched white paper to represent the lightest areas. Practise a few line and tone exercises first.

From strong tonal block into on/off pressure line

MEDIA
• Derwent Graphic: 4B
• Copier paper

Dark silhouette shapes

Strong contrast of dark shape behind light form

Working downwards with pencil marks relating to one another

Forming Line and Tone in Bark

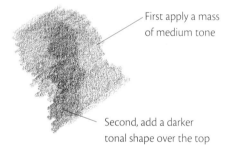

First apply a mass of medium tone

Second, add a darker tonal shape over the top

Next, cut in with a rich dark shape and overlay a series of interesting lines

Include some areas (on the perimeter) of maximum contrast with darkest darks against the lightest light forms

Studying Twig Detail

Find part of a twig with interesting broken areas and study a detail from this.

MEDIA
• Derwent Graphic: 6B
• Copier paper

Practise a directional application exercise to help you understand areas like this – see examples alongside

b)

a)

a) Dot and dash application

On/off pressure lines follow the form of the object

b)

First – tone the shadow recess shape

Build line and tone directionally in relation to the initial shape

Arrows indicate direction of application

Q **Can you demonstrate loosely applied pencil movements with which to start impressions of massed foliage?**

A With a soft 8B or 9B pencil, follow the four steps shown on this page to understand the technique.

1. Create a Tonal Block

Start by making a tonal block, then zigzag along in different directions using varied pressure

2. Develop Your Zigzags

Take your zigzag into short, massed and individual strokes

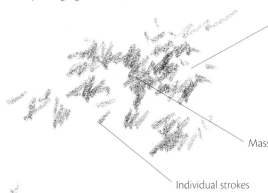

Think of the light (untouched paper) shapes that inadvertently appear while you work as representing light leaves (or flower shapes)

Massed strokes

Individual strokes

3. Create Structure

Take tone 'up to and away' from slim strips – these can then represent structure

Think of these tonal shapes as negative 'shadow recess' areas

After completing an area like this you will have a good, wide, chisel shape on your pencil strip and an alternate fine, narrow side to work with

4. Form a Foliage Mass

Now you can work into your tonal shapes with darker tones behind light forms (creating leaf shapes) to give the impression of a mass of foliage

Alternate fine structure line effects with larger leaf shapes

Q How can I achieve the impression of slim light twigs and branches amidst massed foliage?

A In the process of depicting tonal mass strokes you may occasionally see slim strips of untouched paper. Notice these as they occur and retain them to suggest light twigs and branches.

Tree Study

MEDIA
- Faber-Castell: 6B
- Drawing cartridge paper

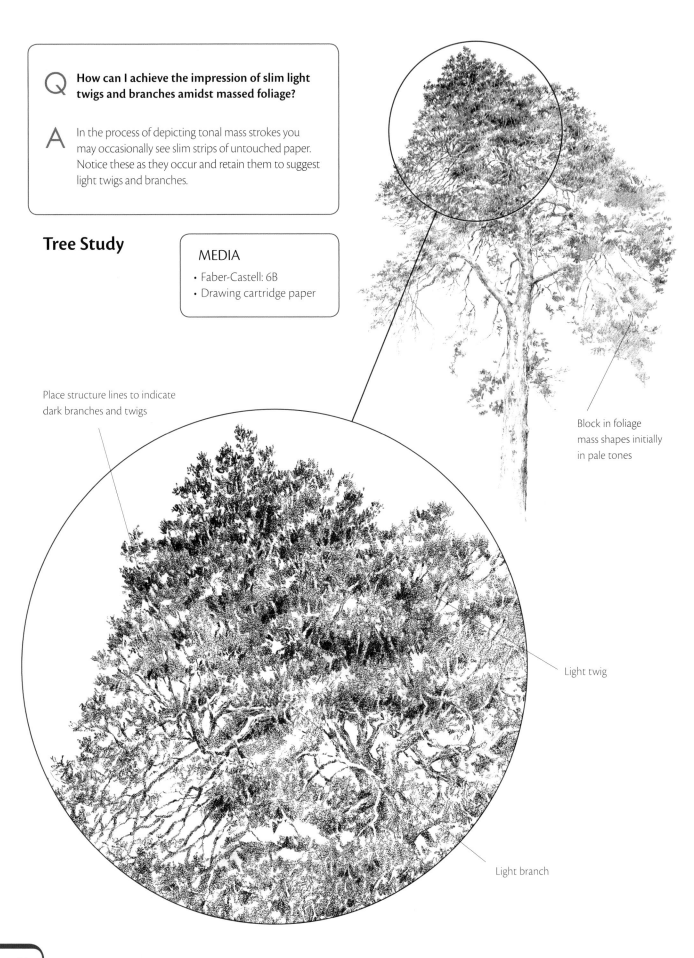

Block in foliage mass shapes initially in pale tones

Place structure lines to indicate dark branches and twigs

Light twig

Light branch

TECHNIQUES: How to Execute the Tree Study

1. Create the Foliage Mass

Using the tip of a sharp pencil, start with the top silhouette shape

Diagram of Stroke Movement

Use a fanned application of small zigzag strokes applied in various directions

Retain any lines of untouched paper – they will represent light twigs/branches amidst dark masses

Work down the tree shape using continuous zigzag movements

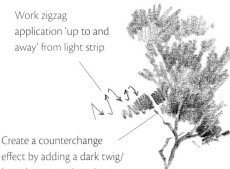

2. Focus on Negative Shapes

Negative shapes between foliage masses need to be retained (as we will see sky through these) – they will receive structure lines crossing them

Working swiftly and loosely will encourage slim untouched paper strips to appear

Work zigzag application 'up to and away' from light strip

Create a counterchange effect by adding a dark twig/ branch as a continuation

3. Create Shadow and Light

A soft pencil pressed firmly on the paper and applied with an erratic movement, twisting the pencil as it moves, will create the start of a shadow side

Complete the branch by adding a delicate 'edge' line

Zigzag movement using firm pressure creates an instant textured impression

Erratically drawn fine lines define the light side of the branch

4. Use a Combination of Strokes

Work across to the light side with zigzag application, lifting the pressure as you travel

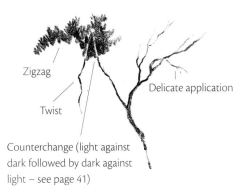

Zigzag

Twist

Delicate application

Counterchange (light against dark followed by dark against light – see page 41)

Detail from a completed image

How can I draw twigs and branches that look convincing?

 Twist the pencil as you work using erratic movements that automatically create angles from which other twigs and branches can emerge.

MEDIA
- Hard pencil
- Bristol board

Skeletal Drawing of a Tree

Make sure some branches pass behind others to form a three-dimensional effect

Introduce angles to create interest and realism

By twisting the pencil and using a zigzag movement, you can automatically create interesting effects

Ensure that cast shadows follow the form of the trunk

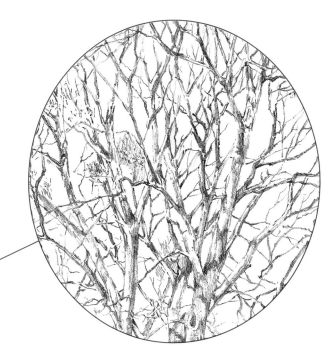

Close-Up of the Central Area

The overall effect may appear complicated. However, if you make sure that all the branches and twigs join their respective supports convincingly, and have regard for their negative shapes, you will achieve a believable skeletal mass.

Remember to place more emphasis on the structures nearest to you with strong contrasts and create a delicate, paler impression for those in the distance.

TECHNIQUES: Branches and Twigs

To create realistic branch and twig forms, simply follow these stages. Before you start, decide which type of pencil you will need to use for the paper type that you are using. A hard grade pencil will form a finer stroke than a softer grade pencil, however it is easier to create shadows using a softer pencil.

MEDIA
- Medium/soft pencil
- Sketchbook paper

When working upwards, twist the pencil as you gently lift it from the paper to create delicate (tapering) tips

Enhance angles

This stroke started at the top, working downwards, using erratic pressure

Create the impression of branches passing behind each other

This erratic up and down (zigzag) application forms the basis for a natural textured effect

TIP *Look for angles in your pencil strokes: it is from these that other twigs may emerge*

How can I create the impression of looking up into an arrangement of branches and twigs?

A Look for negative shapes between branches and suggest recession by using paler tones for distant forms. Notice interesting distortions of bark texture that appear when viewed from this angle.

MEDIA·

- Soft pencil
- Smooth white cartridge paper

Studying Bark Texture

Close observation is required to ensure the correct arrangement of branches

The first stage, comprising positioning of branches and twigs, needs to be as subtle tonal silhouettes in the upper area

Shadow texture indentations can be drawn freely at first before overlays of tone and line explore detail

Tone applied layer on layer will enhance contrasts of shadow shapes

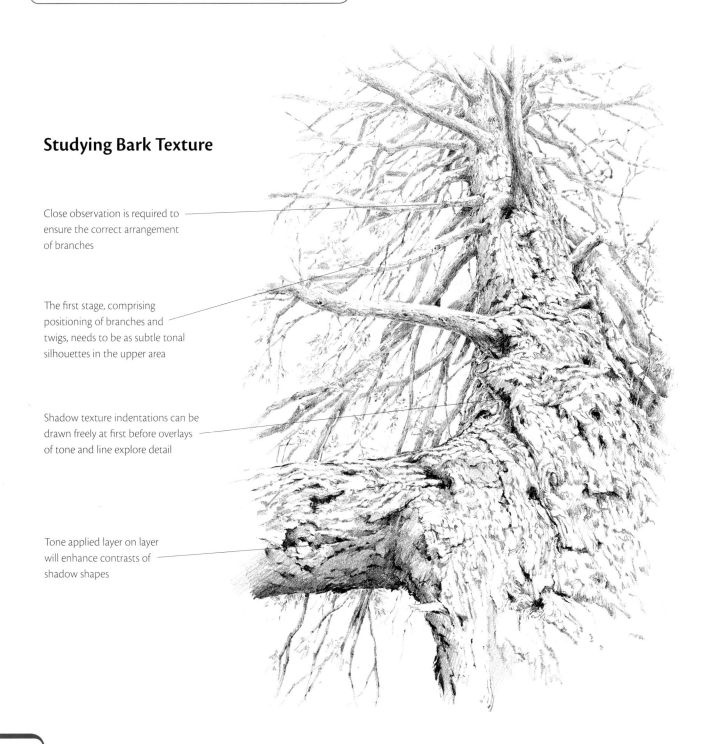

TECHNIQUES: Basic Strokes

The following are key strokes for creating your study of twigs and branches and their methods of application.

1. Loose Application

First pale tone is applied using a zigzag movement

The pencil remains in contact with the paper for this application, which is shown here more widely spaced

2. Up and Down Grazing Movement

Up and down varied pressure movement creates a textured dark form against the light branch in front

Up and down grazing movement creates the initial silhouette shapes

Slim branches may be indicated as textured forms or as different shapes and simple silhouettes

On/off pressure linear marks

3. Diagonal or Contoured Application of Tone

Strong contrasts add drama to the drawing

Initial zigzag using the chisel side of the pencil strip

Twist the pencil as it moves to create the shadow line texture to add interest to the stroke

Twisting the pencil creates delicate shadow lines

Diagonal toning may be overlaid with tonal shapes to indicate the shadow side of the form

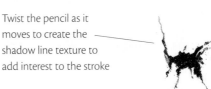

Rich dark shapes start with a zigzag movement

Q What aspects of composition are important considerations for an oval format study?

 A As with most formats, it is important to lead the observer's eye into the composition. In this example, I have used the stream to draw the viewer's eye to an interesting negative shape that relates the main subjects of the tree and wall.

MEDIA
- Soft pencil
- Smooth white cartridge paper

Oval Composition: Landscape Format

When working on this oval study, I started by blocking in tonal shapes before the detailed drawing was overlaid.

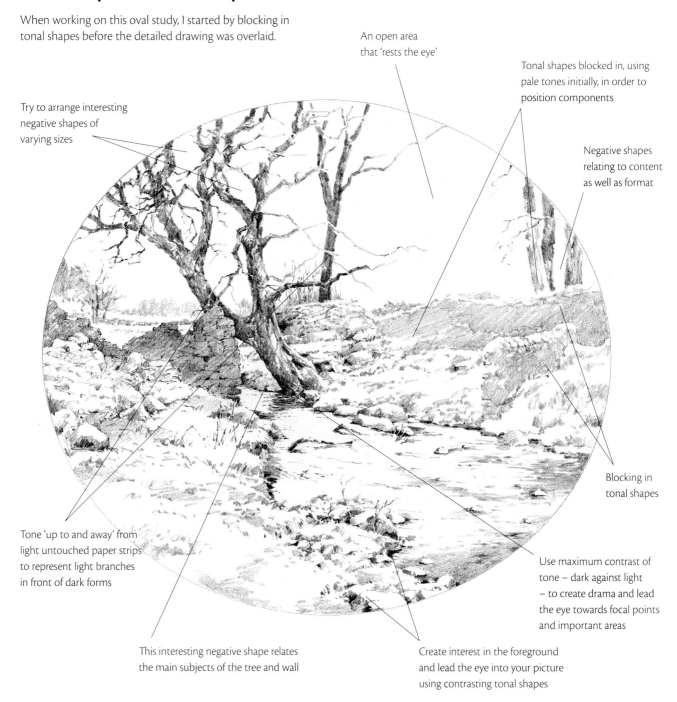

An open area that 'rests the eye'

Tonal shapes blocked in, using pale tones initially, in order to position components

Try to arrange interesting negative shapes of varying sizes

Negative shapes relating to content as well as format

Tone 'up to and away' from light untouched paper strips to represent light branches in front of dark forms

Blocking in tonal shapes

This interesting negative shape relates the main subjects of the tree and wall

Create interest in the foreground and lead the eye into your picture using contrasting tonal shapes

Use maximum contrast of tone – dark against light – to create drama and lead the eye towards focal points and important areas

Oval Composition: Portrait Format

When starting your study, place the first strokes freely with many randomly positioned within the form before enhancing detail using tonal and linear overlays. Remember to vary the direction of application.

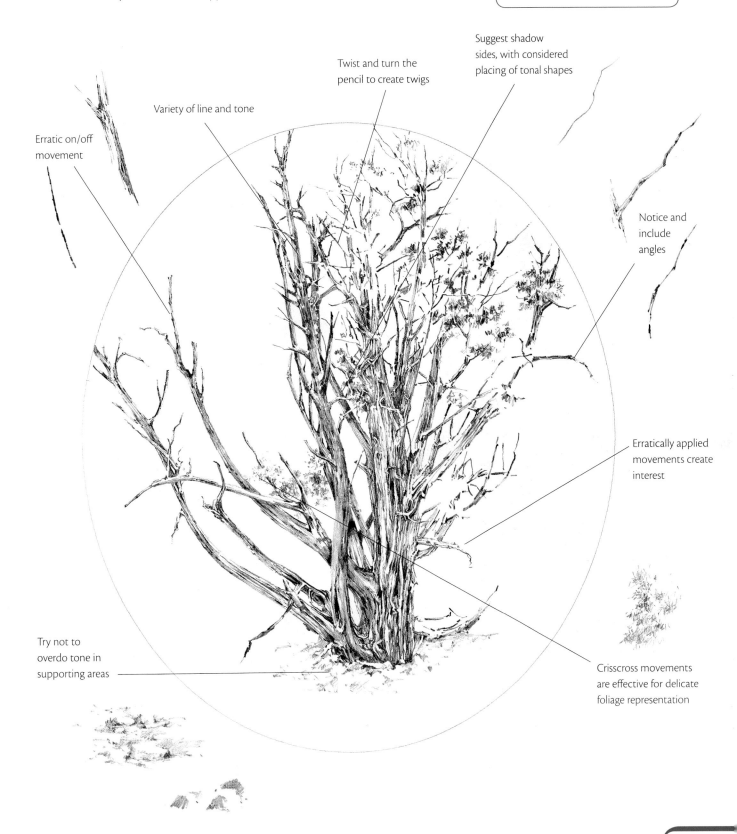

Erratic on/off movement

Variety of line and tone

Twist and turn the pencil to create twigs

Suggest shadow sides, with considered placing of tonal shapes

Notice and include angles

Erratically applied movements create interest

Try not to overdo tone in supporting areas

Crisscross movements are effective for delicate foliage representation

Q Can you explain and illustrate the following, in relation to a woodland scene: a) lost and found, b) counterchange, c) overlaying tone for cast shadows?

A When depicting an area of woodland where we cannot clearly see one tree from another (lost and found), an impression of the scene may be given by drawing detail in some areas and losing it in others. During the first blocking in of tonal shapes you can start establishing areas that appear and disappear when suggesting distant foliage. The examples below and opposite also show counterchange and how tone may be overlaid to create cast shadows.

MEDIA
• Derwent Graphic: HB
• Bristol board

Woodland Scene

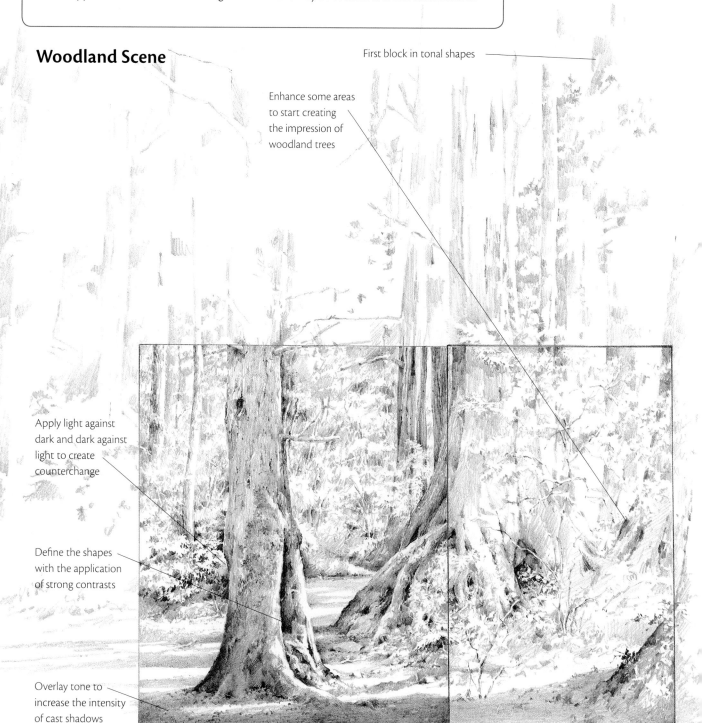

First block in tonal shapes

Enhance some areas to start creating the impression of woodland trees

Apply light against dark and dark against light to create counterchange

Define the shapes with the application of strong contrasts

Overlay tone to increase the intensity of cast shadows

TECHNIQUES: Lost and Found

Lost and found amongst foliage, where we see something clearly in one area and it becomes lost in another, occurs as a result of strong sunlight or cast shadow. Here, the tree trunk is made apparent due to the addition of the cast shadow tone. On the right-hand side, the tree trunk appears to be lost completely.

Counterchange and Overlaying Tone

Counterchange is where we see part of the form as light against dark background (a) and part as dark against light background (b).

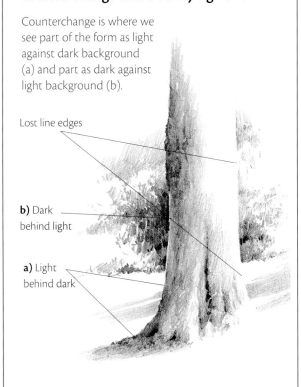

Lost line edges

b) Dark behind light

a) Light behind dark

Overlaying shadow lines

TIP *A variety of tonal values can be achieved, even with a relatively hard grade like an HB, when used on a suitable surface*

Looking at Shadow and Light

In some woodlands standing trees have been carved in situ and they provide an interesting contrast to their neighbours. This example, working from the bottom of the page upwards, demonstrates the importance of shadow and light to bring out the detail in a piece.

Stage 4
Final stage showing intricate detail

This area shows the importance of a strong background tone against the white surface of the paper to bring the light form forward

Stage 3
Gradually more detail is added

Consider lost line edges

Stage 2
Placing a dark background will bring the light side of the form forward

Stage 1
Vertical strokes establish the image and give strength to the representation for the first underdrawing

MEDIA
• Derwent Graphic: HB
• Bristol board

Q **How can I build overlays of tonal values when studying a riverside bank of trees?**

A Consider building the effect in the following five stages:

1. Remembering that untouched (white) paper will represent the lightest lights, position shadow shapes in a pale tone first.

2. Increase the intensity of tone and start defining the light tops of trees by toning 'up to and away' from these areas.

3. Work some detail into the darker shadow recess shapes to create stronger contrasts.

4. Keep working into the detail of areas in shadow while still retaining untouched paper areas that represent lightest areas of foliage.

TIP *For a subject like this it is helpful to use a soft pencil that will blend easily yet create rich dark contrasts. Start by establishing a chisel side to work with by toning a block*

1. First underdrawing establishes positions

2. Overlay tone to increase intensity

MEDIA
- Koh-I-Noor
  Hardtmuth: 7B
- Sketchbook paper

5. Leave the top of the foliage masses as untouched white paper. Tone rich darks up to this top area and lift the pencil pressure to lighten the tone as you move away up into the next light (top) area for subsequent foliage masses.

Create a strip of tonal values before starting work. Remember that those at the extreme ends, when used alongside each other, create maximum contrast to add drama to your study

3. Make light (top) edges crisp by toning a dark behind

4. Work finer details of foliage and structure

GARDENS

Q **There can be so much to take in, visually, in a garden. How can I decide which area to choose and where to start?**

A Choose interesting areas with contrasting shapes, tones and textures. Also look for views containing a variety of forms (see page 48) or smaller details, as shown here.

MEDIA
- Faber-Castell: 6B
- Saunders Waterford HP High White paper

Study of an Area of Interest

Use a viewfinder to choose, and work from, the area of interest outwards. This red line indicates the aperture of the viewfinder. Alternatively, you can opt for cropping: cutting out the area of interest after you have completed a larger area of drawing.

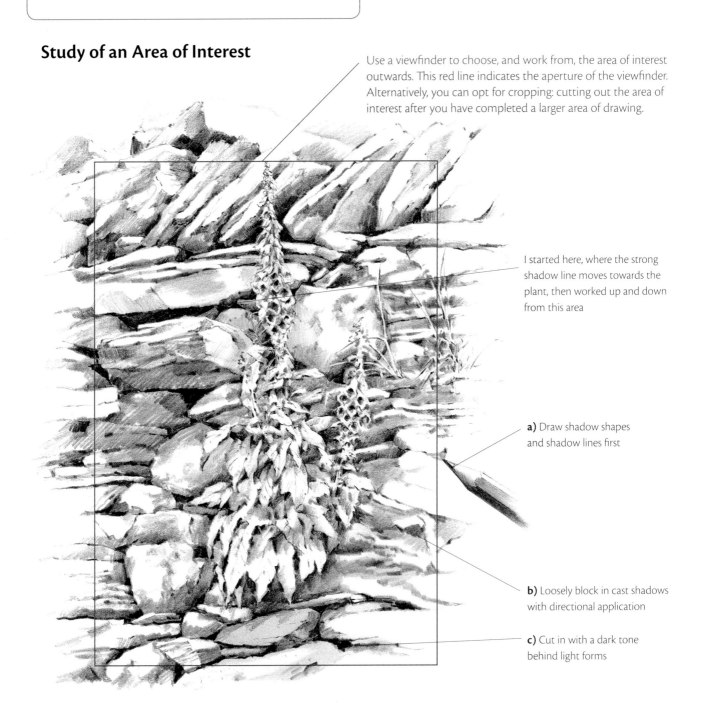

I started here, where the strong shadow line moves towards the plant, then worked up and down from this area

a) Draw shadow shapes and shadow lines first

b) Loosely block in cast shadows with directional application

c) Cut in with a dark tone behind light forms

Experimenting with Format

Mounts may be used with various aperture shapes, and on this page, I have demonstrated three options.

MEDIA

- Faber-Castell: 2B
- Copier paper

Rectangular Format

You could have various aperture shapes cut in one mount to show different views of parts of a garden displayed on the single mount card sheet. Alternatively, a number of drawings of different garden areas could be drawn in a composite arrangement on a single sheet of drawing paper.

Landscape format showing a corner of a garden as seen through a viewfinder

This investigative sketch arranges composition using directional stroke movements

Circular Format

This arrangement, within a circle, encourages the eye to travel into the study.

The left-hand side of the drawing shows how it will be developed and completed

These 'edge' lines will eventually become absorbed by tonal application behind

Darkest dark against lightest light for maximum contrast

Dark tone behind, working 'up to and away' from the light form, brings the stone forward

Tick and flick movement for grasses

These tonal areas indicate how I work 'up to and away' from light edges, to eventually allow them to meet and fill in the shadow area

Gaps are left in the shadow line application to allow for the light structure to cross in front

Initial crisscross stroke movements indicate negative (shadow) shapes

Oval Format

This quick sketch, within an oval format, demonstrates how to avoid the inclusion of too much uninteresting background, allowing the artist and viewer to concentrate on the point of interest.

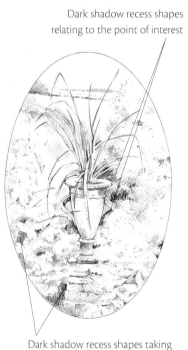

Dark shadow recess shapes relating to the point of interest

Dark shadow recess shapes taking us towards the focal point

Q Can you explain a few pencil stroke movements to help create textures relating to a variety of trees and shrubs in a garden setting with a house?

 A Ornamental trees and shrubs in these settings, with grassy areas and shrub borders may be interpreted without becoming too involved with detail.

MEDIA
- Soft pencil
- Drawing cartridge paper

Developing a House and Garden Setting

Silhouette shape of distant tree using pale (lightly applied) vertical toning

Erratically applied strokes create interesting branches

Regard for silhouette shapes in background areas is important

Toning 'up to and away' from narrow strips of untouched paper suggests light structures amongst dark foliage masses

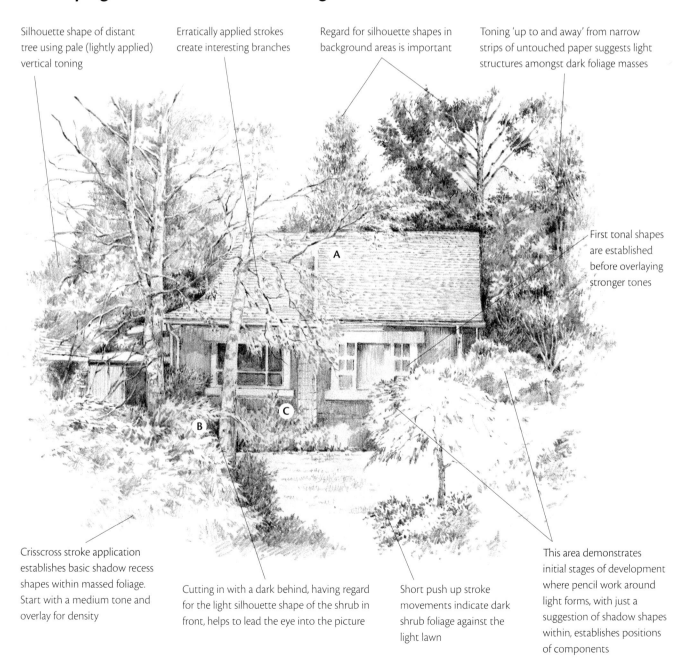

First tonal shapes are established before overlaying stronger tones

Crisscross stroke application establishes basic shadow recess shapes within massed foliage. Start with a medium tone and overlay for density

Cutting in with a dark behind, having regard for the light silhouette shape of the shrub in front, helps to lead the eye into the picture

Short push up stroke movements indicate dark shrub foliage against the light lawn

This area demonstrates initial stages of development where pencil work around light forms, with just a suggestion of shadow shapes within, establishes positions of components

TECHNIQUES: Textures in Foliage

The arrows below indicate the direction in which pencil movements are applied to the paper in order to achieve the varied effects. The three areas featured relate to those indicated in the house and garden study opposite.

Area A

1. Lift pressure to such an extent that only the faintest of lines represents the most delicate of twigs

2. Leave gaps in order to enable the light foliage shapes to appear in front of the building

Area B

3. Dark shadow recess (negative) shape

4. Pull down strokes are placed directionally

5. Look for tonal shapes behind light forms

6. Directionally drawn strokes

7. Vertical toning

8. Blocking in

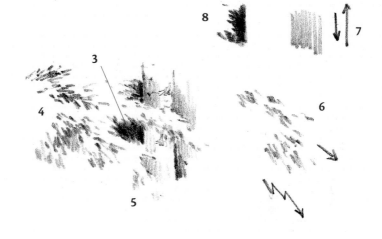

Area C

9. Push the pencil upwards with short movements

10. Zigzag blocking in

11. Vertical zigzags of varied height

12. Vertical toning

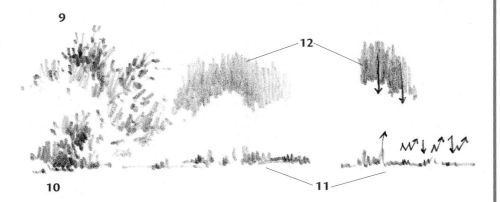

Q How can I depict an interesting themed garden having regard to scale?

 A When you are considering elements of composition, think about the objects within the scene and relate their size appropriately.

MEDIA
- Derwent Graphitone: 4B (solid graphite stick)
- Saunders Waterford HP High White paper

River-Themed Garden

A variety of textures for water, different types of foliage and rocks and stones will add interest to your composition.

The scale and texture of this solid structure contrasts against the soft foliage effects in the background and the open structure of the bridges

A figure on the little bridge indicates the scale of this structure in relation to the surrounding foliage

Reflected images and aquatic plants add interest to the representation of the water's surface

This red arrow shows how the eye is lead into the composition by the arrangement of shapes on either side of the water

The size of this shrub, in relation to the rocks, places it firmly in the foreground

TECHNIQUES: Stone, Foliage and Water Effects

Here are the techniques that I have used to gain a number of different effects, marked A–G on the study opposite, relating to the eight basic strokes on pages 18–21.

Stippling – for Stone Structure

Stippling is a very effective method of accurately representing a rough stone surface, such as on the ornate pillar in the foreground of my composition.

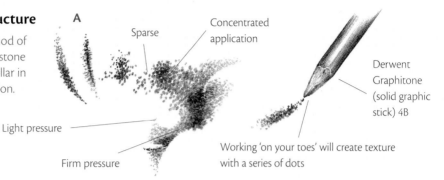

A

Sparse

Concentrated application

Light pressure

Firm pressure

Derwent Graphitone (solid graphic stick) 4B

Working 'on your toes' will create texture with a series of dots

Foliage – for Massed Leaves and Branches

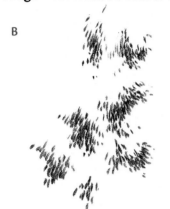

B

'Pull down' strokes (part of movement no. 4)

C

Negative shapes between trees have been created by working 'up to and away' from light strips (trunks) (movement no. 7)

D

a) 'On your toes' to create delicate silhouette of foliage (movement no. 5)

b) Grazing (movement no. 3) fills in tonal areas

Aquatic Plants on Surface Water Effects

E

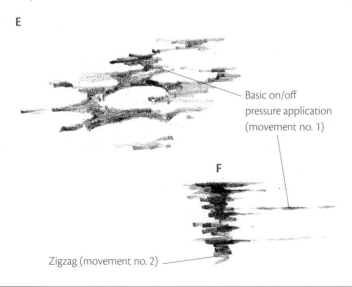

Basic on/off pressure application (movement no. 1)

F

Zigzag (movement no. 2)

Rock Formations

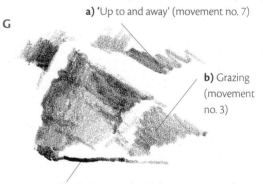

G

a) 'Up to and away' (movement no. 7)

b) Grazing (movement no. 3)

Erratic zigzag and twist (movement no. 2)

Q How can I depict the way plants appear when we are looking down at them amidst stones and rocks?

A Build the images gradually, observing and toning negative shadow shapes first. Gradually add detail to the positive shapes using directional stroke movements, retaining untouched paper for highlighted areas.

MEDIA
- Derwent Graphic: 9B
- Saunders Waterford HP High White paper

Soft Leaves

1. Dark negative 'shapes between' and shadow shapes on, and cast by, leaves have been blocked in lightly first

2. Rich darks have been placed against lightest of the light areas and toned away into a variety of tonal values of the background, creating a three-dimensional effect

3. Final details added

4. Note the direction of cracks between the flagstones in relation to that of cast shadow tone application

5. Leave some areas of untouched paper to represent the lightest lights

TECHNIQUES: Leaves

Using a 9B pencil, make a tonal block to establish a chisel side and a sharp side to the pencil strip

To place dark tone behind light forms work up to the light edge and then away into other background shapes

Zigzag into twist forms the basis of leaf edges for interest of line

Grazing (movement no. 3)

Foliage Amongst Stones

This study uses a harder grade pencil to create more succulent leaves of the plant that contrast against the stony background. Areas A, B and C below highlight the techniques used to start the process and achieve different contrasts and textures.

Avoid too much tonal detail in the highlighted areas

Stones

Rocks

Darkest dark against lightest light for maximum contrast

The basis for the stones on the ground comprises random crisscross areas (movement no. 6)

TIP *To enable the background areas to recede, gently graze a pale tone over the background, 'up to and away' from the light form*

TECHNIQUES: Plants, Rocks and Stones

A. Sweeping strokes

B. Tone 'up to and away' from the light form

C. Crisscross shapes establish the positions of stones at random

Q Can you demonstrate how the treads of steps visually diminish as they recede?

A Depending on our position when viewing steps, the width of the tread will appear to diminish as we look from the area near our feet upwards, towards eye level (see also page 56).

MEDIA
- Derwent Graphitone: 8B
- Saunders Waterford HP High White paper

Step Study in Graphite

Very narrow strip of untouched paper

Strips widen visually as we work down

Untouched paper is retained for lightest areas

Twisting the tip of the graphite stick creates interest for cracks in steps

Pull down strokes, retaining untouched paper for leaf shapes

Vertical grazing

Crisscross application of dark shadow recess shapes within the foliage mass

Further Examples in Graphic Pencil – Relating the Foliage

Shadow and light are essential when forming a step composition. The brilliant white surface of Bristol board enables these strong contrasts to be created using a 5B pencil.

MEDIA
- Derwent Graphic: 5B
- Bristol board

Pull down (directional) strokes

Horizontal grazing for cast shadows over the stone of the steps

For grass, use short up and down strokes, working 'on your toes' (movement no. 5)

This study, as with most step studies, was executed in two stages:

Stage 1: Establishing positions of negative (shadow recess) shapes

Stage 2: Building the foliage mass

Flagstone joints lead the viewer's eye towards the steps

53

Q How can I create an impression of leaves and twig structures behind and against a solid object in the garden?

A Establish, in pale tones, the position of the object then loosely indicate tonal shapes 'up to and away' from the form – as shown opposite. You can then draw in finer details to relate the background to the object.

MEDIA

- Faber-Castell: 8B
- Smooth surface quality cartridge paper

Watering Can Study

Ferns require more delicate strokes of dark tones cutting in around the light form

Option Two: Working into tonal areas, leaving white paper for the lightest lights

Option One: See the demonstration opposite

Dark structure across light form

Initial diagonal placing of parallel line toning on which other tonal layers are built

Options for Depicting Leaf Shapes and Twig Structure

Start by looking at negative shapes and work tone around light forms (the positives). Then tone gently across the light forms that you want to recede or to receive cast shadows. Two options are demonstrated here:

Option One: Continuous Wandering Line

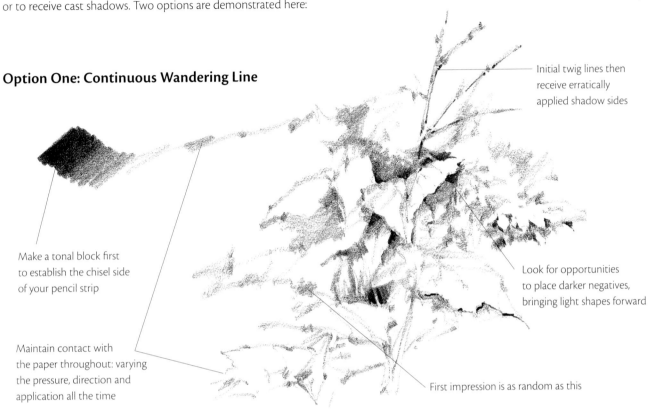

Initial twig lines then receive erratically applied shadow sides

Make a tonal block first to establish the chisel side of your pencil strip

Look for opportunities to place darker negatives, bringing light shapes forward

Maintain contact with the paper throughout: varying the pressure, direction and application all the time

First impression is as random as this

Option Two: Individually Placed Negative and Silhouette Tonal Shapes

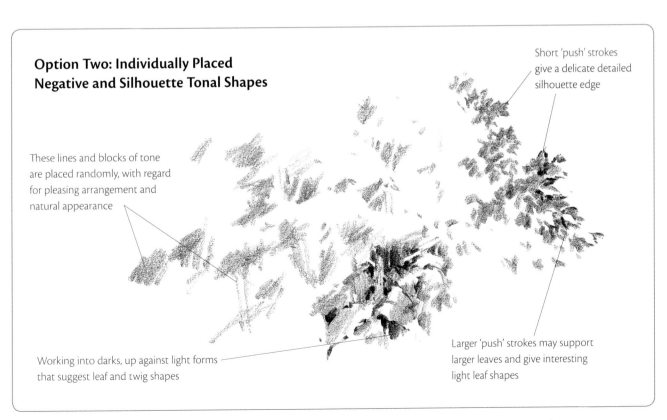

Short 'push' strokes give a delicate detailed silhouette edge

These lines and blocks of tone are placed randomly, with regard for pleasing arrangement and natural appearance

Working into darks, up against light forms that suggest leaf and twig shapes

Larger 'push' strokes may support larger leaves and give interesting light leaf shapes

Q How can I work out perspective angles and ellipses for a group of plant containers?

A I have arranged these containers on steps in order to explain various perspective angles.

Preliminary Sketch

Red lines demonstrate how all the lines would eventually meet at the vanishing point beyond the drawing when the steps are seen at this perspective angle.

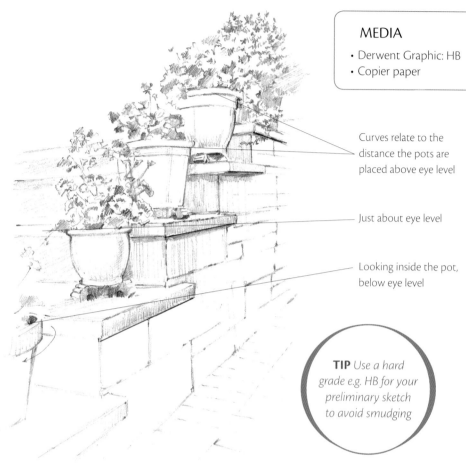

MEDIA
• Derwent Graphic: HB
• Copier paper

Curves relate to the distance the pots are placed above eye level

Just about eye level

Looking inside the pot, below eye level

TIP *Use a hard grade e.g. HB for your preliminary sketch to avoid smudging*

Investigative Sketch

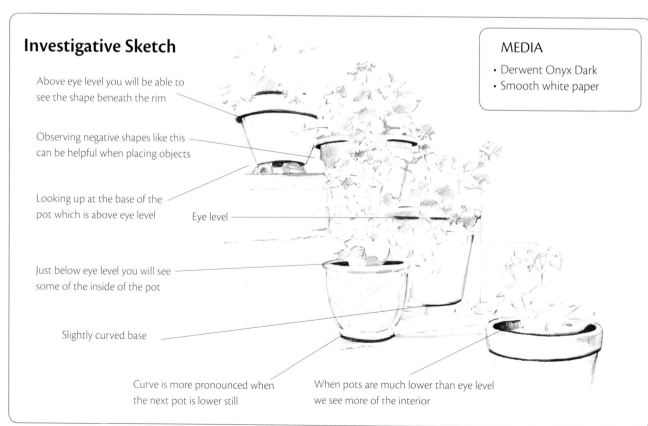

MEDIA
• Derwent Onyx Dark
• Smooth white paper

Above eye level you will be able to see the shape beneath the rim

Observing negative shapes like this can be helpful when placing objects

Looking up at the base of the pot which is above eye level

Eye level

Just below eye level you will see some of the inside of the pot

Slightly curved base

Curve is more pronounced when the next pot is lower still

When pots are much lower than eye level we see more of the interior

Applying Tone

MEDIA
- Derwent Sketching: 8B (water-soluble)
- Bristol board

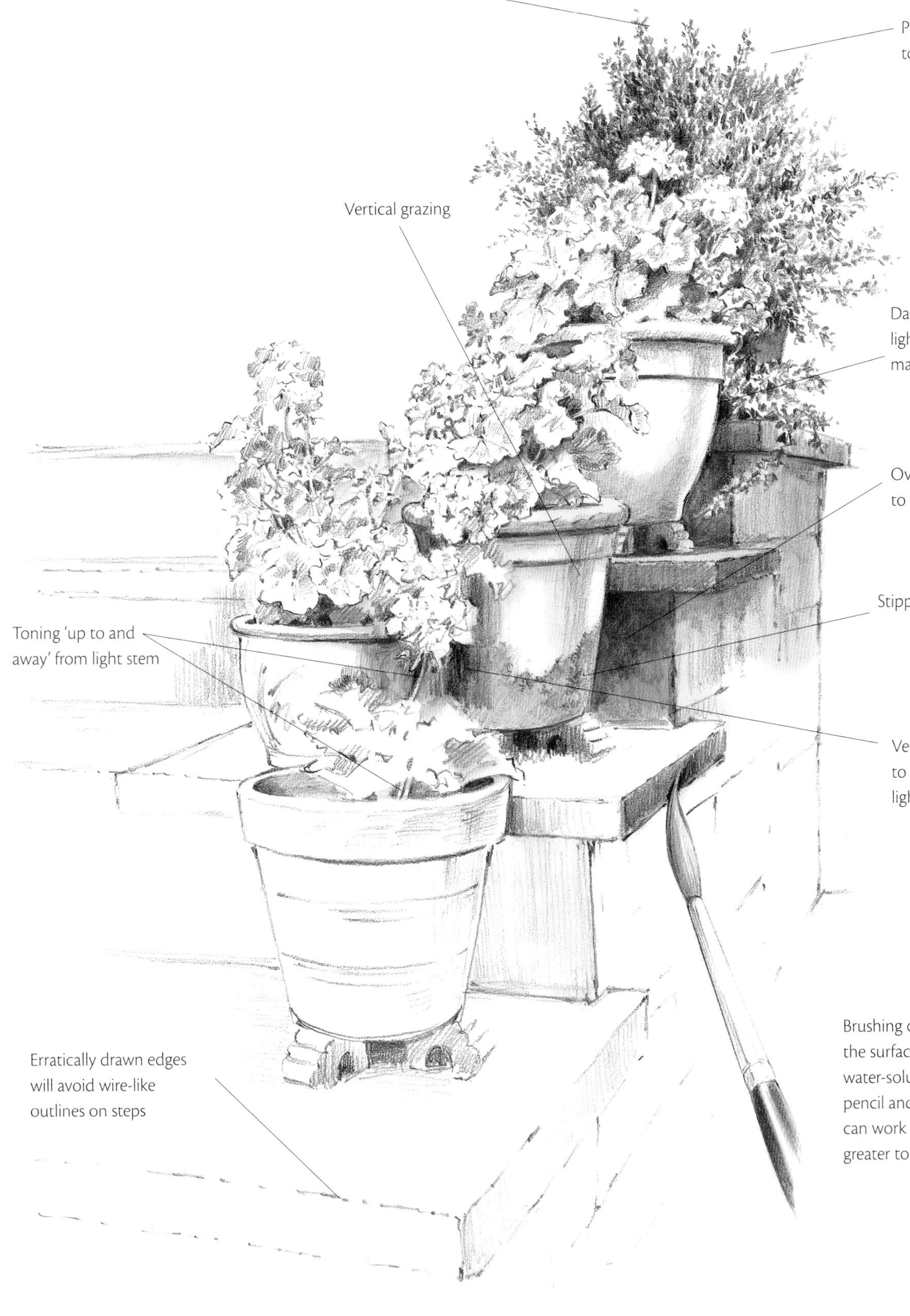

Simple silhouette shape

Put, push, pull strokes to represent tiny leaves

Vertical grazing

Darkest dark against lightest light for maximum contrast

Overlaying tone to enrich darks

Stippling for texture

Toning 'up to and away' from light stem

Vertical grazing 'up to and away' from light form

Erratically drawn edges will avoid wire-like outlines on steps

Brushing clean water across the surface will blend this water-soluble graphite pencil and, when dry, you can work over this for greater tone enhancement

Q **How can I apply the personal grid method to drawing blooms?**

A If you are working from one of your own photographs, you can place a sheet of tracing paper over the image and look for 'V' shapes from which to draw the guidelines.

MEDIA
• Derwent Graphic: B
• Copier paper

Rose

Draw guidelines on tracing paper over your photo image. Try to draw your guidelines freehand, without using a ruler. You can check for accuracy afterwards and alter if necessary.

Draw the guidelines that you see on the tracing paper overlay actually on your first study. This will help you to make comparisons and achieve accuracy

A small 'shape between' like this is very helpful (the shape between the guideline and parts of two petals)

Look for a suggestion of veins to help you apply pencil strokes directionally to follow the form

Interesting on/off pressure edge line

Shadow shape

Notice how closely A and B line up. This often happens and it is a great help when the 'V' shapes do this

Let your investigative toning lines follow the form

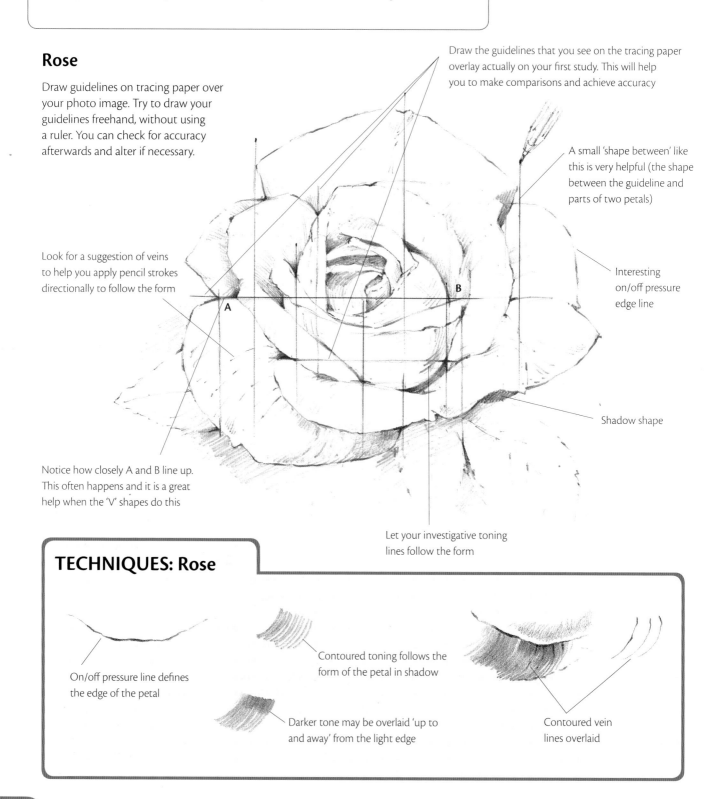

TECHNIQUES: Rose

On/off pressure line defines the edge of the petal

Contoured toning follows the form of the petal in shadow

Darker tone may be overlaid 'up to and away' from the light edge

Contoured vein lines overlaid

Dahlia (Ball)

The beauty of blooms like this may still be enjoyed and appreciated without the use of colour, as monochrome representations employ the drama of tonal contrasts.

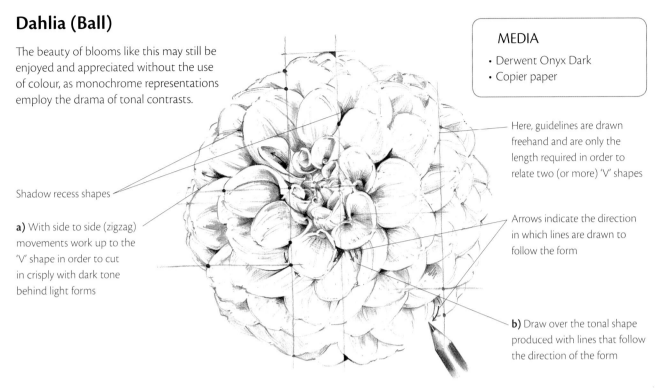

Here, guidelines are drawn freehand and are only the length required in order to relate two (or more) 'V' shapes

Shadow recess shapes

a) With side to side (zigzag) movements work up to the 'V' shape in order to cut in crisply with dark tone behind light forms

Arrows indicate the direction in which lines are drawn to follow the form

b) Draw over the tonal shape produced with lines that follow the direction of the form

Dahlia (Banker)

With both concave and convex shapes in this flower head there is plenty of variety with which to create an interesting study. The media used are ideal for smooth petal interpretation, incorporating rich darks that contrast with untouched paper (lightest light) areas.

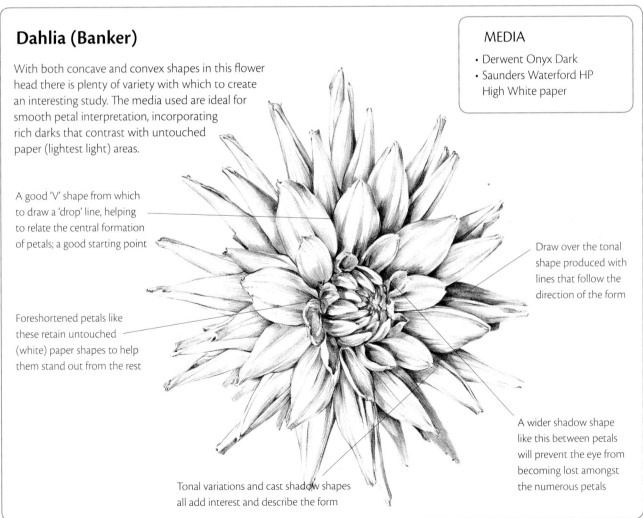

A good 'V' shape from which to draw a 'drop' line, helping to relate the central formation of petals; a good starting point

Draw over the tonal shape produced with lines that follow the direction of the form

Foreshortened petals like these retain untouched (white) paper shapes to help them stand out from the rest

A wider shadow shape like this between petals will prevent the eye from becoming lost amongst the numerous petals

Tonal variations and cast shadow shapes all add interest and describe the form

STILL LIFE

 Q How can I make an exercise, such as drawing this old shoe, interesting?

 A Place it amongst different textures, for example a variety of leaves and stones, as if found in a garden.

MEDIA
- 3B pencil
- Drawing cartridge paper

Study of a Shoe in Foliage

When you compare the basic depiction of a shoe (above) with the study in foliage (below), it is clear to see how placing your object in a setting immediately adds interest to your piece. Start by positioning pale tonal shapes over the form of the shoe to suggest where foliage will cross in front. Then accentuate light forms and increase the tone behind them, allowing white paper to remain and indicate highlighted areas.

TIP *See page 54 for foliage techniques to use when drawing vegetation over the shoe*

Create strong contrasts

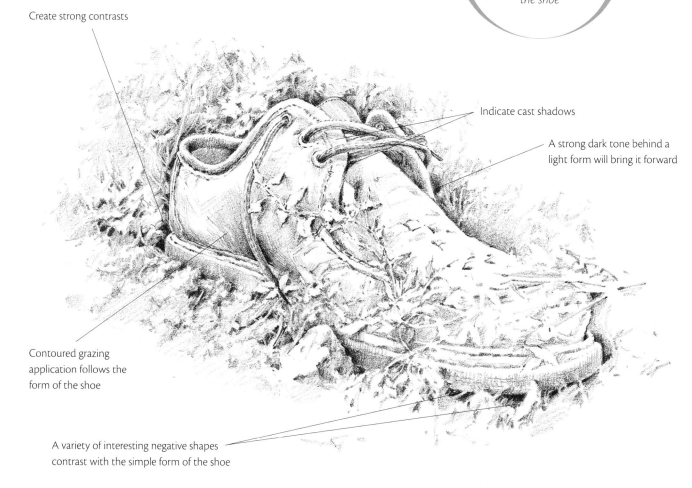

Indicate cast shadows

A strong dark tone behind a light form will bring it forward

Contoured grazing application follows the form of the shoe

A variety of interesting negative shapes contrast with the simple form of the shoe

Sketching the Shoe

First Investigative Sketch

Before you include a background, you firstly need to make an investigative sketch of the shoe, using guidelines to help place components in relation to each other.

MEDIA
• B pencil
• Copier paper

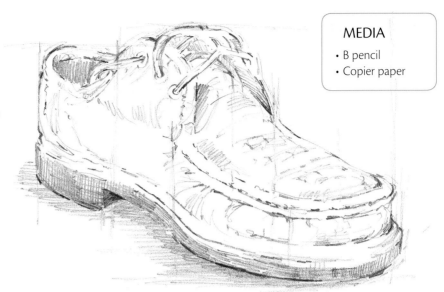

TECHNIQUES: Basic Shoe

The following techniques have been used to depict the basic shoe image:

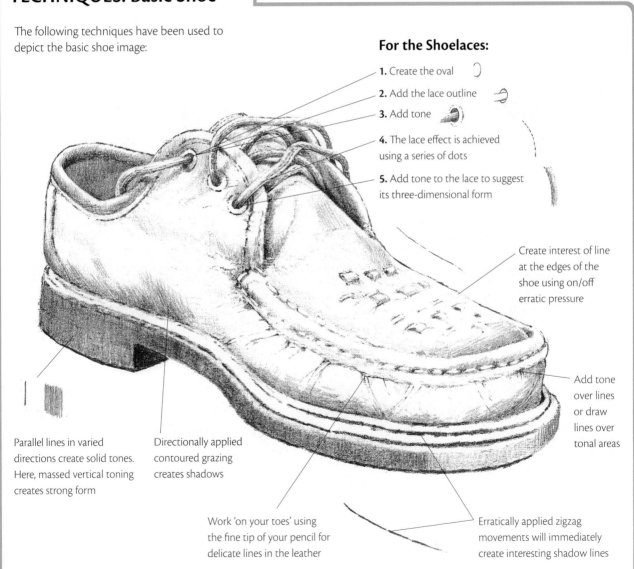

For the Shoelaces:

1. Create the oval

2. Add the lace outline

3. Add tone

4. The lace effect is achieved using a series of dots

5. Add tone to the lace to suggest its three-dimensional form

Create interest of line at the edges of the shoe using on/off erratic pressure

Add tone over lines or draw lines over tonal areas

Parallel lines in varied directions create solid tones. Here, massed vertical toning creates strong form

Directionally applied contoured grazing creates shadows

Work 'on your toes' using the fine tip of your pencil for delicate lines in the leather

Erratically applied zigzag movements will immediately create interesting shadow lines

Q Can you explain the difference between an investigative sketch and a detailed drawing?

A In an investigative sketch, the artist is literally investigating the subject by looking at the structure and arrangement of components, using guidelines and wandering lines that find the form (see below). On the opposite page, you can compare this with a detailed drawing.

MEDIA
- HB pencil
- Copier paper

Investigative Sketch of a Group of Vegetables

A hard-grade pencil is useful for the initial sketch, as it is less likely to smudge when gently travelling over the paper to find forms with directionally placed strokes. Also, the vertical and horizontal guidelines can be slender and not interfere with detailed observation.

TIP Introduce tone into your investigative sketch, rather than restricting your drawing to outlines only, and work within the forms

Look for 'V' shapes and think of these as visual contact points through which guidelines may be drawn to help you place components correctly in relation to each other

You can see how this vertical 'drop' line places the tip of the carrot accurately in relation to the onion above

'Open' negative

'Closed' negatives

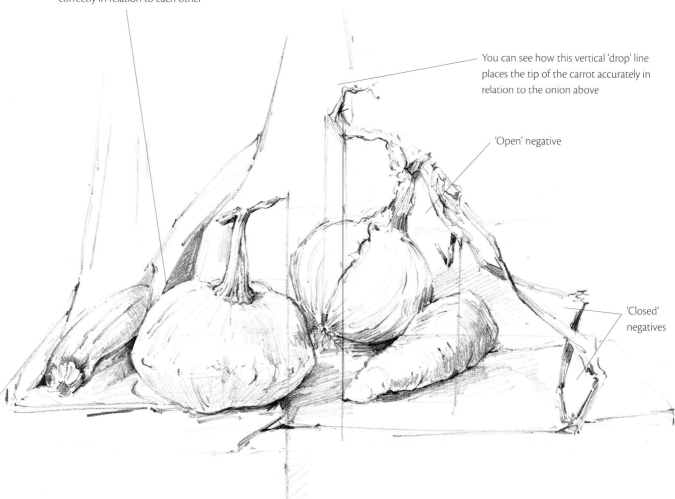

Detailed Drawing of a Parsnip

This detailed drawing shows the resulting image from an
initial investigative sketch where the main elements have
been traced from the sketch, omitting guidelines and other
rough marks, for a representational depiction.

MEDIA
- Faber-Castell: B
- Drawing cartridge paper

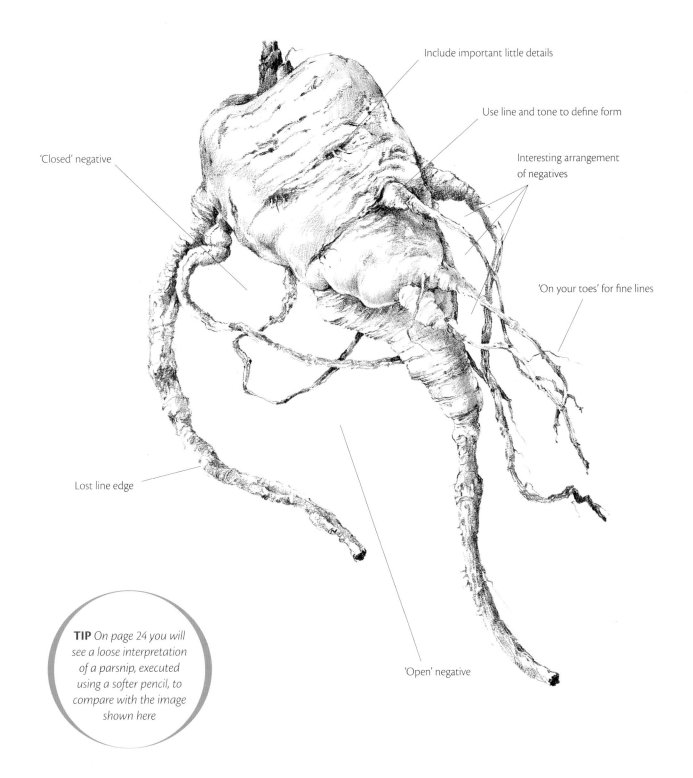

Include important little details

Use line and tone to define form

Interesting arrangement
of negatives

'On your toes' for fine lines

'Closed' negative

Lost line edge

'Open' negative

TIP *On page 24 you will
see a loose interpretation
of a parsnip, executed
using a softer pencil, to
compare with the image
shown here*

Can you suggest a simple still life subject that requires a variety of different techniques?

 A single or couple of cupcakes require a variety of effects and I have demonstrated these on two different papers.

MEDIA
- Derwent Graphic: 6B
- Drawing cartridge paper

Preliminary Sketch

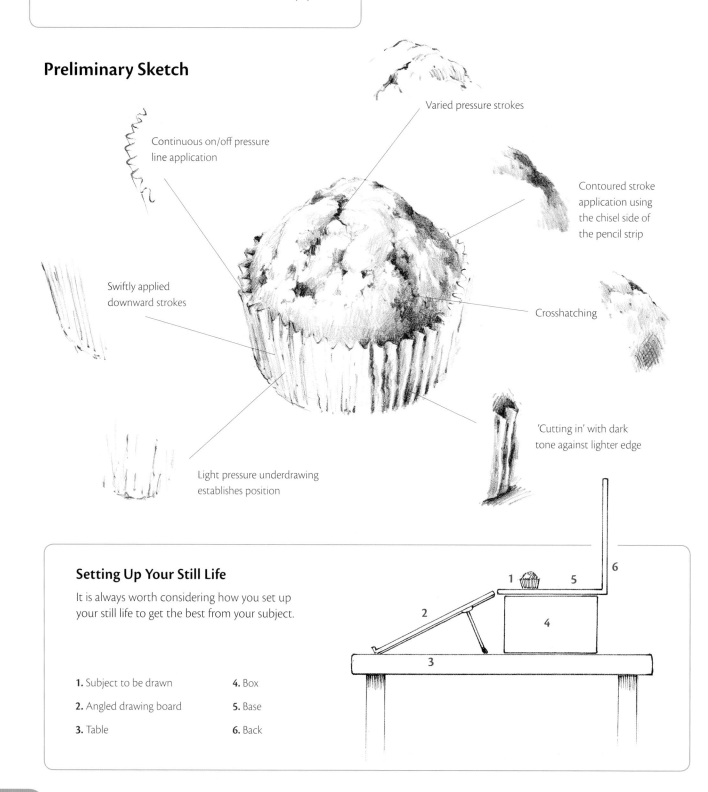

Varied pressure strokes

Continuous on/off pressure line application

Contoured stroke application using the chisel side of the pencil strip

Swiftly applied downward strokes

Crosshatching

'Cutting in' with dark tone against lighter edge

Light pressure underdrawing establishes position

Setting Up Your Still Life

It is always worth considering how you set up your still life to get the best from your subject.

1. Subject to be drawn

2. Angled drawing board

3. Table

4. Box

5. Base

6. Back

Final Sketch

MEDIA
- Koh-I-Noor Hardtmuth 1500: 8B
- Saunders Waterford HP High White paper

TIP For bold, free strokes on larger drawings use a soft pencil and, for more intricate detail, a harder grade

TECHNIQUES: Cupcake

A. For cast shadow formed, use a flat tonal overlay to increase intensity

B. To give texture to the surface of the cake towards the light, use stippling

C. For the shadowed surface of the cake, draw in with dark tone over directionally placed undertone

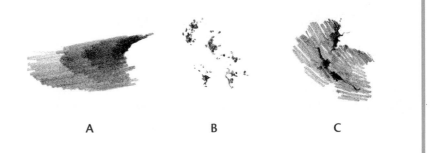

A   B   C

> **Q** **What can I learn from drawing a common object like a folded umbrella?**
>
> **A** It is interesting to compare parts of a simple object like this to a variety of other subjects.

> **MEDIA**
> • Soft pencil
> • Textured paper

Detailed Drawing of an Umbrella

Four areas of this object have been annotated below. Solid objects have been covered on pages 60–65. However by studying the other three; folded cloth, gathered fabric and cord, there is much to learn.

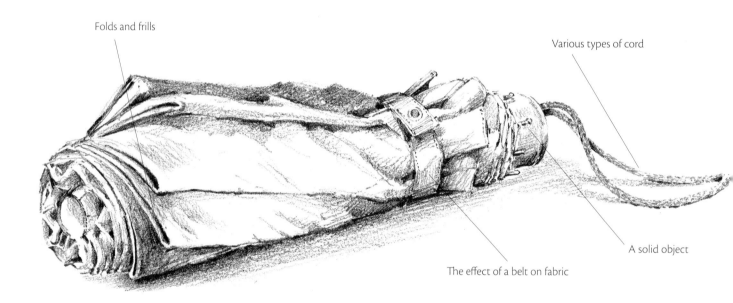

Folds and frills

Various types of cord

A solid object

The effect of a belt on fabric

TECHNIQUES: Studying Different Types of Cord

Here, I have used a 6B and 8B pencil to study the different patterns found in cord.

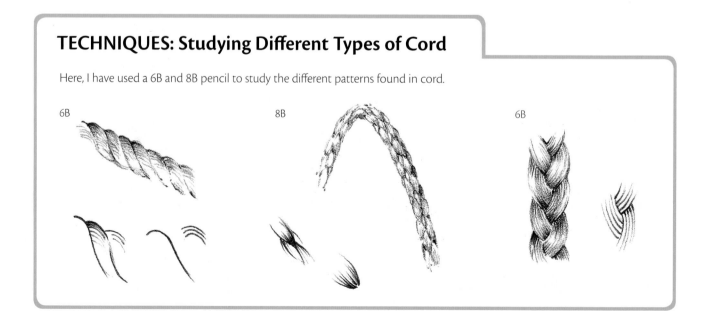

6B

8B

6B

TECHNIQUES: Studying Folds in Fabric

The folds of the umbrella are similar to the fabric drapes found in a hanging curtain or the gathers of material around a belt.

TIP *Try different pencil brands and grades to find which works best for your style, paper and for the specific subject you have decided to draw*

Heavy draped fabric

Soft gathered fabric

Similar effect to heavy draped fabric (above)

Similar effect to belted garment (above)

How can I use soft toys to help me understand the use of guidelines in relation to fabric?

 These two beanbag bears have been arranged in a way that demonstrates negative shapes, strong contrasts and interesting fabric folds in this investigative sketch from life.

MEDIA
• Graphite
• Copier paper

TIP Include all your 'working out' lines and tones on your preliminary drawing so that you can eventually trace off only the lines that you need to establish the essentials on your good paper

Using Guidelines: Beanbag Bears

In this investigative sketch, you can see how a personal grid of vertical and horizontal guidelines helps relate the bears to one another.

A 'drop line' from the edge of the ear lines up with the shadow shape of the shoulder area below

The line passing from the edge of the ear relates to that of the tip of the paw below

Red dots show the value of horizontal guideline relationships

A 'drop line' from a point in the fold of the cloth of the background lines up with the heel of the bear

This horizontal guideline relates the shoulder and paw of the nearest bear to the other bear's arm

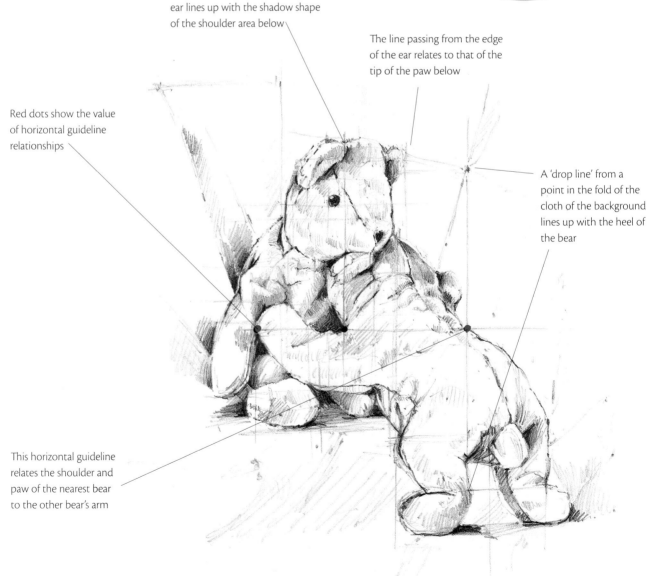

Using a Preliminary Drawing as the Basis for Coloured Work

This coloured study of the beanbag bears illustrates how the guidelines made in your preliminary sketch can help to shape and improve your final study.

MEDIA
- Watercolour pencils
- Tinted Bockingford watercolour paper

Folds in the background cloth are useful in that they provide visual contact points from which to place guidelines

A good angle (contact point) from which to 'drop' a guideline

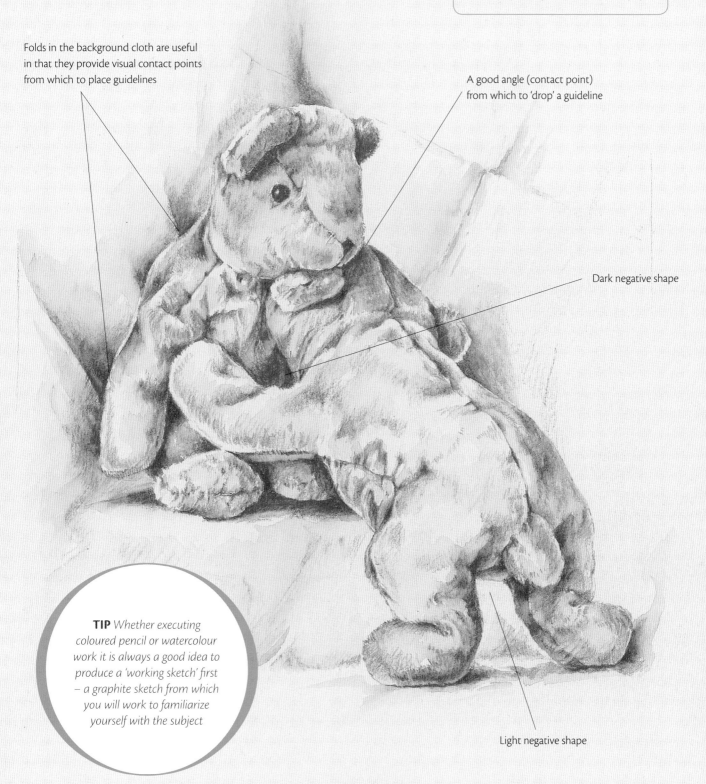

Dark negative shape

TIP *Whether executing coloured pencil or watercolour work it is always a good idea to produce a 'working sketch' first – a graphite sketch from which you will work to familiarize yourself with the subject*

Light negative shape

Q How can I overlay tones to achieve strong contrasts of tonal values and textures using basic stroke application, with consideration for the direction in which the strokes are placed?

A Consider the direction in which your fingers would move over the surface of a form and tone your drawing with strokes that follow that direction.

MEDIA
- Graphite
- Copier paper

Toning Directionally

I have drawn arrows to indicate my consideration for various directions and have shown how tonal strokes follow contours of form.

A. Receptacle

B. Casing

C. Curved surface

D. Flat surface

E. Short rim

F. Curve of rim

G. Large flat area into a contoured finish

H. Contoured side of flat surface

Using Strong Contrasts for Firm Directional Application

Machine parts and tools present a more interesting composition when softened by being placed on rag or, as here, partially embedded in sand (see also page 72).

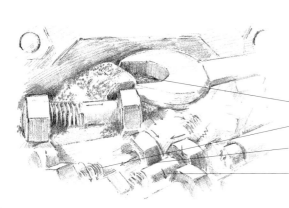

Look for tonal shapes

'Feel' your way around the form

Strong contrasts

Arrows indicate direction in which line and tone are applied, with a regard for the form they represent

Final Drawing

Intensity of tone is increased layer on layer until the darkest darks contrast against untouched white paper for maximum effect. A variety of textured surfaces, with their individual treatments, create added interest.

A. 'Pull down' strokes – vertical grazing – for shadow side of flat form

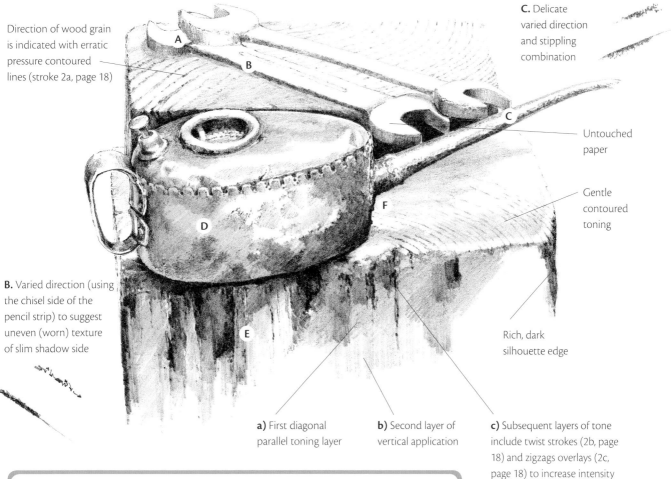

C. Delicate varied direction and stippling combination

Direction of wood grain is indicated with erratic pressure contoured lines (stroke 2a, page 18)

Untouched paper

Gentle contoured toning

B. Varied direction (using the chisel side of the pencil strip) to suggest uneven (worn) texture of slim shadow side

Rich, dark silhouette edge

a) First diagonal parallel toning layer

b) Second layer of vertical application

c) Subsequent layers of tone include twist strokes (2b, page 18) and zigzags overlays (2c, page 18) to increase intensity and add texture

TECHNIQUES: Overlaying Tones

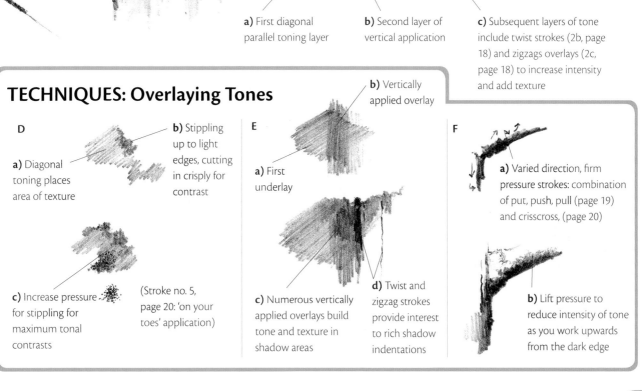

D

a) Diagonal toning places area of texture

b) Stippling up to light edges, cutting in crisply for contrast

c) Increase pressure for stippling for maximum tonal contrasts

(Stroke no. 5, page 20: 'on your toes' application)

E

a) First underlay

b) Vertically applied overlay

c) Numerous vertically applied overlays build tone and texture in shadow areas

d) Twist and zigzag strokes provide interest to rich shadow indentations

F

a) Varied direction, firm pressure strokes: combination of put, push, pull (page 19) and crisscross, (page 20)

b) Lift pressure to reduce intensity of tone as you work upwards from the dark edge

Q **How can I create interest in a still life that includes shells?**

A Some shells are so intricate that there is enough interest of line and tone within the form to create a study from a single image.

MEDIA
• Derwent Inktense Outliner
• Copier paper

TIP Make sure your application follows the form of the shell

Seaside Study

Content: Mirror Tile
Small pile of builders' sand
Selection of pebbles
Rusty old chain
Shells

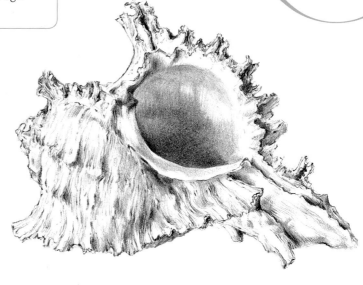

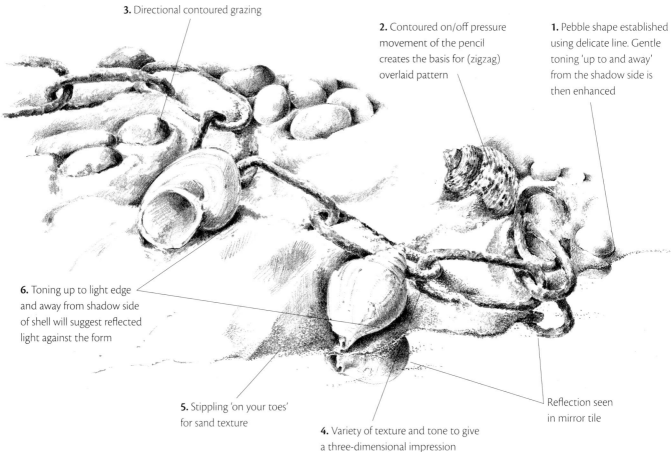

3. Directional contoured grazing

2. Contoured on/off pressure movement of the pencil creates the basis for (zigzag) overlaid pattern

1. Pebble shape established using delicate line. Gentle toning 'up to and away' from the shadow side is then enhanced

6. Toning up to light edge and away from shadow side of shell will suggest reflected light against the form

Reflection seen in mirror tile

5. Stippling 'on your toes' for sand texture

4. Variety of texture and tone to give a three-dimensional impression

TECHNIQUES: Basic Strokes

1. On/Off Pressure Stroke (page 18)

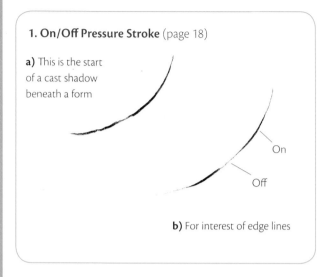

a) This is the start of a cast shadow beneath a form

On

Off

b) For interest of edge lines

2. Erratic Pressure Stroke (page 18)

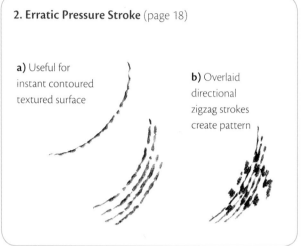

a) Useful for instant contoured textured surface

b) Overlaid directional zigzag strokes create pattern

3. Grazing Application (page 19)

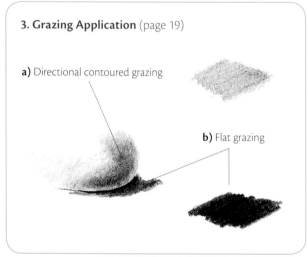

a) Directional contoured grazing

b) Flat grazing

4. Put, Push, Pull Application (page 19)

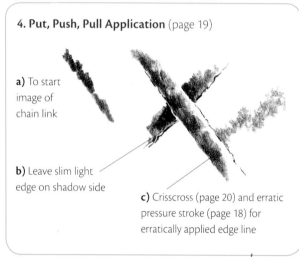

a) To start image of chain link

b) Leave slim light edge on shadow side

c) Crisscross (page 20) and erratic pressure stroke (page 18) for erratically applied edge line

5. 'On Your Toes' Application (page 20)

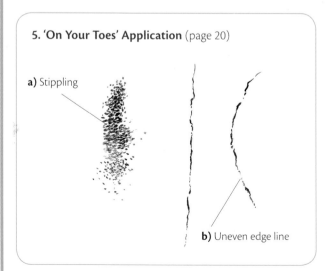

a) Stippling

b) Uneven edge line

6. 'Up to and Away' Movement (page 21)

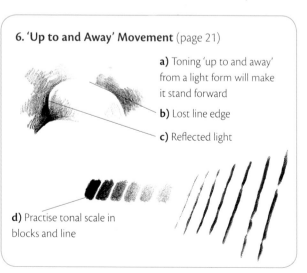

a) Toning 'up to and away' from a light form will make it stand forward

b) Lost line edge

c) Reflected light

d) Practise tonal scale in blocks and line

Q Can you explain and demonstrate a simple four-step process showing:

1. A first 'rough' (investigative) drawing and variety of marks used

2. How a tracing of this would look before starting to fill in the tonal shapes

3. How to start building tonal values

4. How the final drawing appears with strong tonal contrasts?

 A This study of a group of vegetables has been broken down into four stages to demonstrate how a study develops.

MEDIA
• Derwent Graphic: B
• Copier paper

1. The Investigative Sketch

This first 'rough' drawing uses a variety of lines to explore the subject.

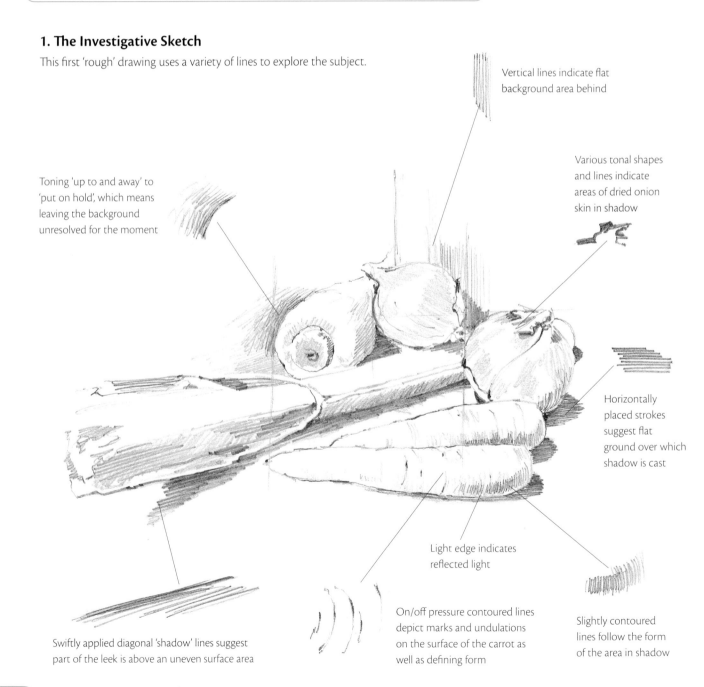

Vertical lines indicate flat background area behind

Various tonal shapes and lines indicate areas of dried onion skin in shadow

Toning 'up to and away' to 'put on hold', which means leaving the background unresolved for the moment

Horizontally placed strokes suggest flat ground over which shadow is cast

Light edge indicates reflected light

Slightly contoured lines follow the form of the area in shadow

Swiftly applied diagonal 'shadow' lines suggest part of the leek is above an uneven surface area

On/off pressure contoured lines depict marks and undulations on the surface of the carrot as well as defining form

2. Tracing the Study

Here, I am demonstrating how a tracing from a rough drawing positions objects within a group on new sheet of paper; the second stage of the drawing process.
You can trace using tracing paper, a window or the light box method.

Lost line

Area in shadow

Area of cast shadow

Interesting on/off pressure line indicates edge of form

Lines placed with regard for position of veins on leek

3. Beginning to Build Tonal Values

Prior to building tonal values, it is important to place areas in shadow and indicate areas of cast shadow.

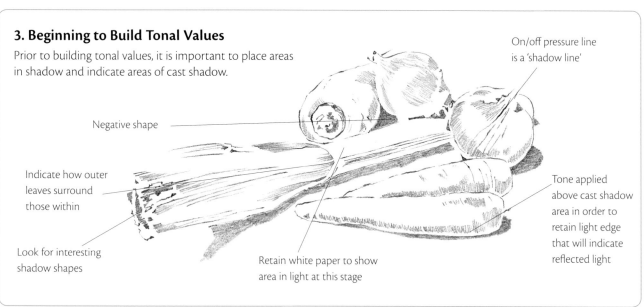

On/off pressure line is a 'shadow line'

Negative shape

Indicate how outer leaves surround those within

Look for interesting shadow shapes

Retain white paper to show area in light at this stage

Tone applied above cast shadow area in order to retain light edge that will indicate reflected light

4. The Final Drawing

Here in the final drawing, shadows and highlights are indicated with regard for tonal values to create a detailed representational image.

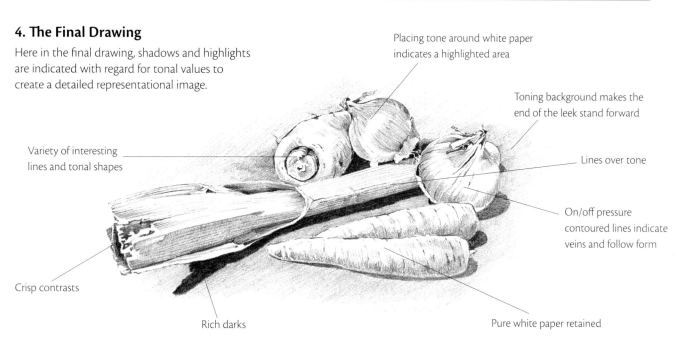

Placing tone around white paper indicates a highlighted area

Toning background makes the end of the leek stand forward

Variety of interesting lines and tonal shapes

Lines over tone

On/off pressure contoured lines indicate veins and follow form

Crisp contrasts

Rich darks

Pure white paper retained

BUILDINGS

Q What strokes can I use to sketch the essence of a building quickly without depicting too much detail?

A Erratically applied lines and vertical or diagonal toning create an impression of the building without adding in too much detail. The techniques opposite demonstrate some of the stroke movements used.

MEDIA
- Derwent Graphic: 2B
- Drawing cartridge paper

Study of a Complex Building

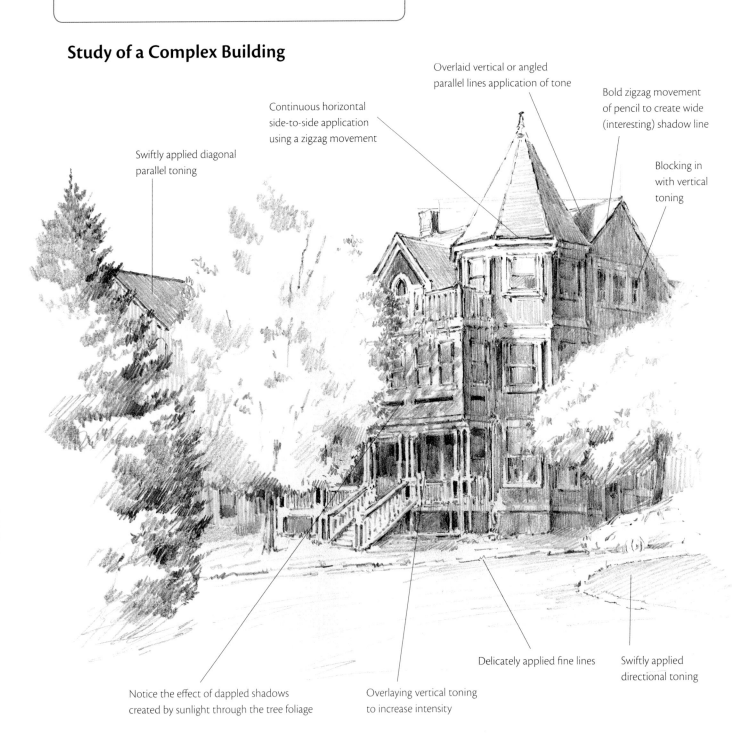

Overlaid vertical or angled parallel lines application of tone

Bold zigzag movement of pencil to create wide (interesting) shadow line

Continuous horizontal side-to-side application using a zigzag movement

Blocking in with vertical toning

Swiftly applied diagonal parallel toning

Notice the effect of dappled shadows created by sunlight through the tree foliage

Overlaying vertical toning to increase intensity

Delicately applied fine lines

Swiftly applied directional toning

Initial Guideline Sketch

Before starting on the final sketch of a building it is useful to carry out a quick guideline sketch simply to position windows and so on in relation to other components.

TECHNIQUES: Complex Building

Practise line and tone application to create the essence of a building following these techniques:

Focusing on Tone

1. Start with a tonal block

2. Lift pressure

3. Create a vertically applied block of tone

4. Overlay darker tone

5. Draw lines over tone

Line Application

6. Feint guidelines may be drawn initially to position components (see guideline sketch above)

7. Vary the pressure on the pencil to create interest of edge and for detail in linear application

8. Tone away from the edge line to indicate contrast between the dark and light sides of the building

Lines are firmly placed over initial guidelines as the sketch develops

9. Interest of line and tone

10. Blocking in a tonal shape over an initial linear underlay

Zigzag Application

11. Broad zigzag application to create wide shadow line

12. This shows how zigzag application starts, before overlaying widens the shadow line

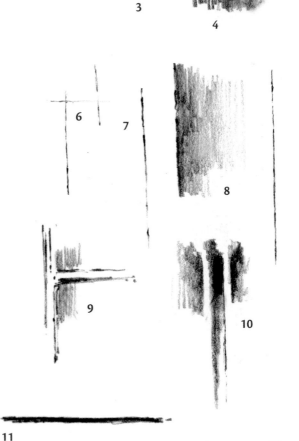

Q **How can I create the effect of cast shadows over various surfaces on a building?**

 A The techniques opposite explain how to apply cast shadows to tiles, brickwork, woodwork and other materials.

MEDIA
- Derwent Graphic: 4B and B
- Drawing cartridge paper

Creating a Cast Shadow Effect: House Study

The cast shadow areas of this study were initially placed in a pale tone to indicate positions. Subsequent layers of tone then enrich the depth of shadow.

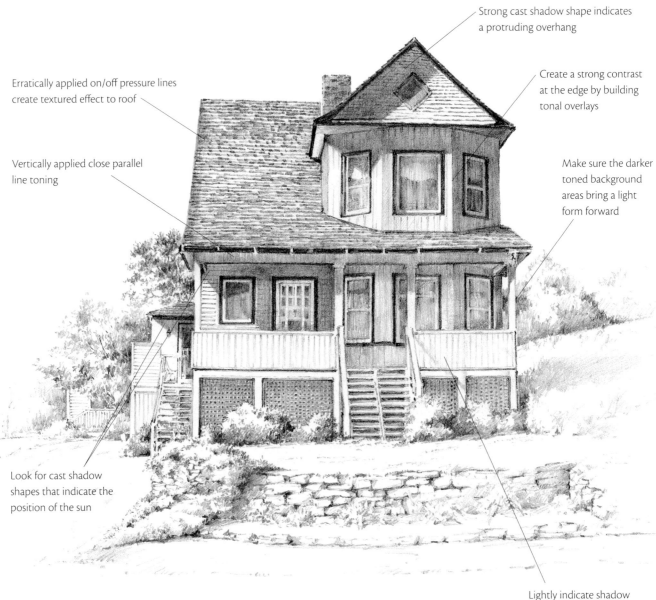

Strong cast shadow shape indicates a protruding overhang

Create a strong contrast at the edge by building tonal overlays

Erratically applied on/off pressure lines create textured effect to roof

Make sure the darker toned background areas bring a light form forward

Vertically applied close parallel line toning

Look for cast shadow shapes that indicate the position of the sun

Lightly indicate shadow lines of the screen

TECHNIQUES: Windows, Roof and Woodwork

The following techniques demonstrate how cast shadow effects may be achieved for various parts of your house study:

Windows

1. Apply soft pencil e.g. 4B or 5B, for the initial dark tone

2. Vertically applied close parallel lines toned to create cast shadow shape

3. Neaten the edges using a harder grade, e.g. B

4. Applying a variety of tones indicates curtains behind the glass

Roof

1. Erratic on/off pressure parallel strokes indicate the texture of the roof

2. Erratic line application adds interest to any vertical or horizontal boarding

Woodwork

Step 1:

1. Counterchange on supporting posts

2. Tone 'up to and away' from a light post to bring it in front of a dark shadow recess behind

Step 2:

1. Cut in below an overhang and up to the edge of a post

2. Tone horizontally below the overhang

3. Keep overlaying tones, using the same vertical application, until you have achieved the desired tone. Then overlay vertical tonal lines to achieve density

Walls and Window Frames

Tonal Exercise:

1. Start with a vertically applied tonal block

2. Move along, using less pressure to achieve even, paler tone

3. Diagonal overlay

1. Toning 'up to and away' from light edge

2. Indicate a blind by placing darker tone beneath

3. Vertical toning for a flat surface

Q **Can you demonstrate how effects of pencil grades and paper surfaces work together for stonework representations showing cast shadows and shadow recess shapes?**

A Windows of ancient buildings are excellent subjects for discovering how the use of strong tonal contrasts and the retention of untouched white paper can create drama when depicting shadows against and within stonework.

MEDIA
• Bristol board

Experimenting with Brands and Grades of Pencil

Before you begin, it is good to try line and tone using different brands of pencil and a variety of grades on various surfaces. Discover which one you feel comfortable with to represent your subject. These examples demonstrate the difference between brands and grades.

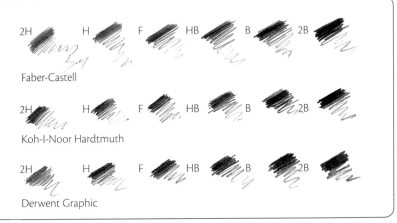

2H H F HB B 2B
Faber-Castell

2H H F HB B 2B
Koh-I-Noor Hardtmuth

2H H F HB B 2B
Derwent Graphic

Toning a Study

This drawing shows how the study started with a wandering line positioning the components along with pale tonal shapes, prior to overlaying more tone 'up to and away' from the light edges. Diagonally applying parallel toning established the shadow sides of the forms. The retention of white paper provided maximum contrast and drama.

1. Initial drawing of stonework is light and loose in line and tone

2. Fine line drawing contrasts with strong tonal shapes

3. Diagonal toning swiftly places areas of cast shadow

4. Feint edge line up to which tone is placed to fill in the dark background

5. Dark tone is worked 'up to and away' from the light form

6. Untouched paper is retained to indicate areas in full sunlight

Final Study

This study shows the combinations of soft grade pencil on textured paper in applying tone to create the drama of intense darks and shadow lines with more texture than is apparent when working on the smoother surface of Bristol board (shown opposite).

MEDIA
• Soft pencil
• Drawing cartridge paper

1. Maximum contrast – darkest dark against lightest light – will bring a light form forward

2. Wandering lines establish the positions of stones

3. Diagonally applied toning in shadow areas

4. Overlaying tone to build intense darks

a) Medium tone is loosely applied to fill in the recess shape initially

b) Darker tone is overlaid to increase density

5. On/off (varied pressure) stroke indicates shadow line

Q How can I use intensity of tone effectively to indicate dark interiors and shadow sides of stone buildings?

A You can either draw the stonework in a linear way and lay tone over the top, or tone the shadow areas first and draw into them.

MEDIA
- Derwent Graphic: 6B
- Drawing cartridge paper

First Sketches

In my first sketches on this page (and on page 27), the shadow side of the building has received vertical toning over a few linear marks, suggesting stonework.

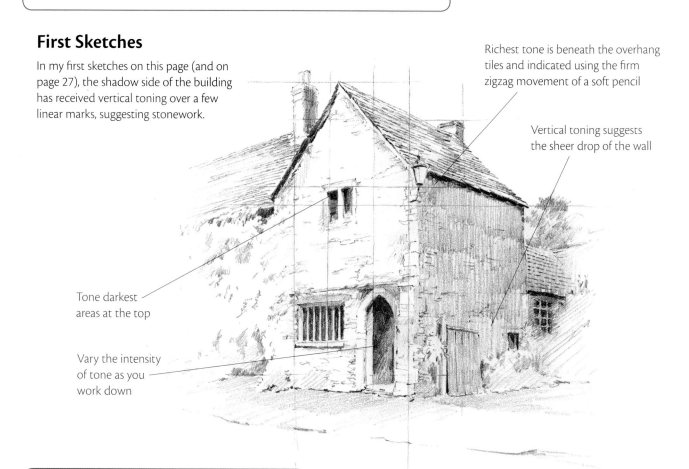

Richest tone is beneath the overhang tiles and indicated using the firm zigzag movement of a soft pencil

Vertical toning suggests the sheer drop of the wall

Tone darkest areas at the top

Vary the intensity of tone as you work down

TECHNIQUES: Applying Tone

Techniques for toning and drawing over tone are as follows:

Stone and Stonework:

1. **a)** Shadow lines between stones

   b) Shadow tone overlaid

2. **a)** Shadow tone placed first

   b) Shadow lines drawn in over tonal layer to indicate stonework

Doorway Area:

Cut in with dark tone first and work down into lighter tones

Tile Overhang:

a) Zigzag movement applied using the chisel side of a soft pencil

b) Indicate uneven tile overhang with angled shadow lines between tiles

c) Graze down, away from dark zigzag line, using horizontal strokes to indicate cast shadow

Completed Study

In this completed study, you can see how effective these techniques are, where overlaying line and tone (respectively) will enable you to create contrasts of tone and texture to represent various surfaces and shadow recesses.

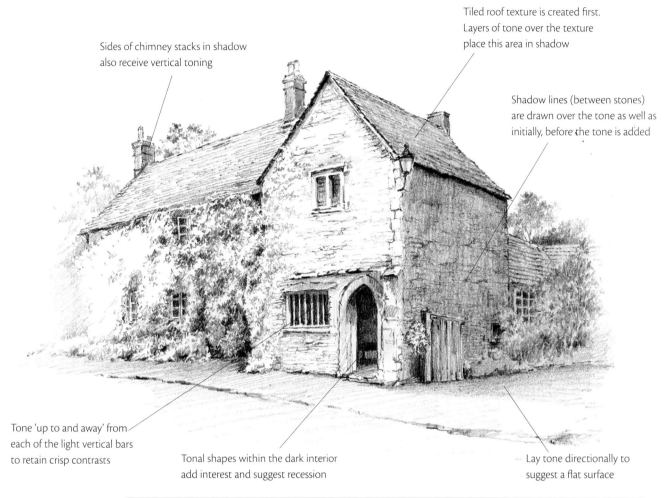

Sides of chimney stacks in shadow also receive vertical toning

Tiled roof texture is created first. Layers of tone over the texture place this area in shadow

Shadow lines (between stones) are drawn over the tone as well as initially, before the tone is added

Tone 'up to and away' from each of the light vertical bars to retain crisp contrasts

Tonal shapes within the dark interior add interest and suggest recession

Lay tone directionally to suggest a flat surface

Cottage Study

Here is another example of a building with stone walls in shadow.

Darkest dark at the top of the opening creates the strongest contrast in this area

Strong contrast of light against dark on the corners brings these areas forward

Q What different stroke movements can I use to represent the contrasting textures of wooden rails and the combination of wood and stone for steps against a log cabin?

 A Use erratic line application for studies of wood and dark tonal shapes between the smoother textured stones and use a paper that will help you to achieve interest of tone.

MEDIA
- Derwent Graphitone: 8B
- Drawing cartridge paper

Log Cabin Study

Textures created using a soft graphite stick for a grainy effect add interest to subjects such as wood, stone and foliage.

This soft graphite stick, used on slightly textured cartridge paper, creates interest within the tonal area for a grainy effect

Blocking in the shadow recess shapes within foliage masses

Initial blocking in of negative shapes between wooden planks and slats

Zigzag and twist movements of sharpened (8B) graphite stick, using firm pressure, creates interesting shadow lines

Overlaying vertical grazing movements will build tonal density and allow the light forms to stand forward

Gently tone 'up to and away' from the light side of the form and make the edge line interesting using erratic pressure movements

TECHNIQUES: Wood and Stone

It is useful to focus on a small area containing textures of wood and stone, such as this step setting, to perfect your technique.

TIP *Try Graphitone on a variety of papers and discover the interesting effects that can be achieved when working on textured surfaces*

For details, sharpen the graphite stick to a fine point

Toning 'up to and away' from light side of form creates contrast and brings light form forward

Note the variety of effects in this small area alone

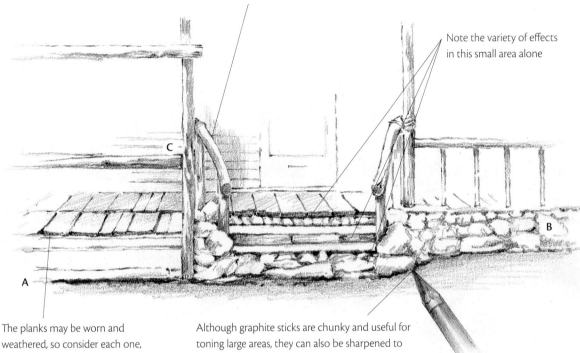

The planks may be worn and weathered, so consider each one, and how it lays, individually

Although graphite sticks are chunky and useful for toning large areas, they can also be sharpened to a fine point when required for detailed work

A. An erratic pressure combination of zigzag (for wider shadow lines) and twist of the stick (for narrower shadow lines) creates interest within planks, boarding and log walls etc.

B. Stones are individually placed in relation to one another using wandering lines, before the dark shadow recess shapes are introduced

C. Erratic line movement over (and with) the application of tone immediately creates the effect of the textured surface of supporting posts

Q **How can I create a 'free' (spontaneous) impression of a derelict building using graphite blocks?**

A Use the block at various angles to the paper, alternating the wide end with the narrow sides and points of corners to achieve marks of different shapes and widths to represent various aspects of your interpretation.

Derelict Building

Twist the block slightly between your fingers as you use varied pressure directionally drawn strokes to represent trunks, branches and twigs

Vary pressure placed on the block as you work up and down to create the soft impression of background in the distance

Use the entire side of the block end, placed vertically, to suggest planks of wood and boarding (the block may be broken in two for ease of application)

Firm pressure: long or short vertical strokes will create rich dark tones for shadow shapes and other dark areas

Varied direction strokes, requiring different pressure placed on the end of the block, will create an impression of clumps of weeds

Work more 'on your toes' using the corner of the block for the fine effect needed to depict conifers in the distance

MEDIA
• Derwent soft graphite block
• Drawing cartridge paper

Sweeping strokes using gentle pressure on the block end will suggest undulations of ground

Firm pressure zigzags followed by directional irregular lines create dark edges to grassy areas

Q I understand that when we draw we are only making marks but how can I know which marks to make and how to use them in my drawings?

 A Just look at the tonal shapes. Forget the subject while you relate the shapes to each other within your composition. Try not to include everything you see, and ask yourself the question: 'how much can I leave out without losing the essence of the interpretation?'

MEDIA
- Derwent Graphic: 6B
- Smooth white cartridge paper

Looking at Marks and Shapes

Make your marks varied and interesting. Contrast shapes, textures and tones while being selective as to what you choose to include and leave out.

This shows how the marks appear when enlarged – just as simple shapes

A series of vertical marks seen as being in sunlit and shadowed areas are all that is needed to indicate content of walls

This suggestion informs the viewer that a window is there, even though the image is not complete

What you leave out is just as important as what is included, as long as you relate the shapes created around the light area to the subject, in this instance water ripples

Q **Using a building as source material, how can I create an abstract interpretation?**

A There are many ways of doing this and the one I have demonstrated here shows my initial drawing of the reflections from other buildings seen on a glass-fronted building. Taking one of the distorted images viewed between the frame of glazing bars, I worked on textured paper, using and developing the tonal marks and shapes to create an abstract interpretation.

Studying Abstract Shapes

Observing part of the whole study in detail offers the opportunity to experiment with executing tonal values and techniques and for the use of imagination regarding image shapes and textures.

A variety of curves contrasting with dramatic presentation of horizontal lines

Tone fading out into the white paper

Lost line edge

An interesting 'shape between' for the area of untouched paper and its relationship with the format (or mount)

Variety of tonal and linear shapes

Crisp contrasts

Contrasts of rich dark and medium tones against brilliant white

Q **How many stages may be involved in the drawing of a completed building?**

A Most of my studies of buildings can be completed with three key stages, as explained below and opposite.

MEDIA
- Derwent Onyx Dark
- Saunders Waterford HP High White paper

TECHNIQUES: Stages for Drawing a Building

The first investigative drawing may be executed on copier or layout paper. You can position components and make changes as you work.

Stage 1: Investigative Sketch or Drawing

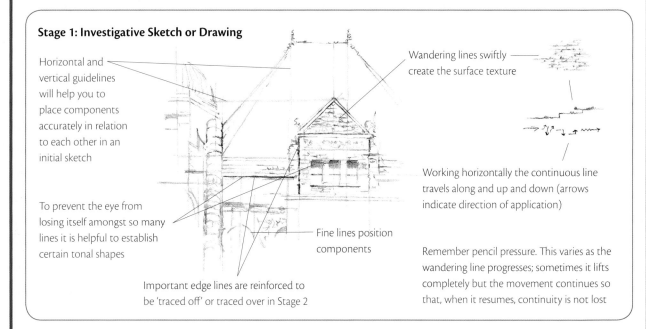

Horizontal and vertical guidelines will help you to place components accurately in relation to each other in an initial sketch

To prevent the eye from losing itself amongst so many lines it is helpful to establish certain tonal shapes

Important edge lines are reinforced to be 'traced off' or traced over in Stage 2

Fine lines position components

Wandering lines swiftly create the surface texture

Working horizontally the continuous line travels along and up and down (arrows indicate direction of application)

Remember pencil pressure. This varies as the wandering line progresses; sometimes it lifts completely but the movement continues so that, when it resumes, continuity is not lost

Stage 2: Placing Simple Outlines

Trace off the important edge lines onto good paper. They are seen as dark lines on the demonstration drawing, whereas you will need them to be much paler for them to be absorbed into your final drawing.

Stage 3: Toning the Details

To establish a horizontal shadow line of some width draw a short line, go back over the last little bit and then move forward into another short line (a). Repeat until the line is complete using the wide (chisel) side of the pencil strip (b). Build up tone for the completed image (c)

a)

b)

c)

Detail from completed image

The Three Stages of a Building Study

Stage 1
Investigative sketch using guidelines and wandering line application. A loose interpretation enables you to adjust certain elements.

Stage 2
Tracing off simple (feint) structure lines to position the components, on which the tonal drawing will be built.

Stage 3
Completing image by toning the details to establish strong contrasts.

Stage 1
Foreground images need only be indicated swiftly to establish position at this stage – no detail is necessary

Stage 2
First edge lines need to be paler than this – tone is overlaid to build intensity gradually

Stage 3
Work 'up to and away' from edges to fill in darker recessed areas by overlaying tonal lines and shapes

Q What techniques can I use to represent accessories like a hat and glasses as well as clothing?

A Whether you are portraying a profile, three-quarter view or full face, it is a good idea to execute an investigative guideline sketch first and then work this into a loosely drawn pencil sketch before reaching the final study. Follow the guidelines below for tips on how to depict realistic accessories on a figure.

MEDIA
- Faber-Castell: 6B
- Copier paper

Second Stage: Pencil Sketch

These loosely drawn sketches allow you to experiment with placing the accessories and look at different angles before starting your final study.

First Stage: Investigative Drawing

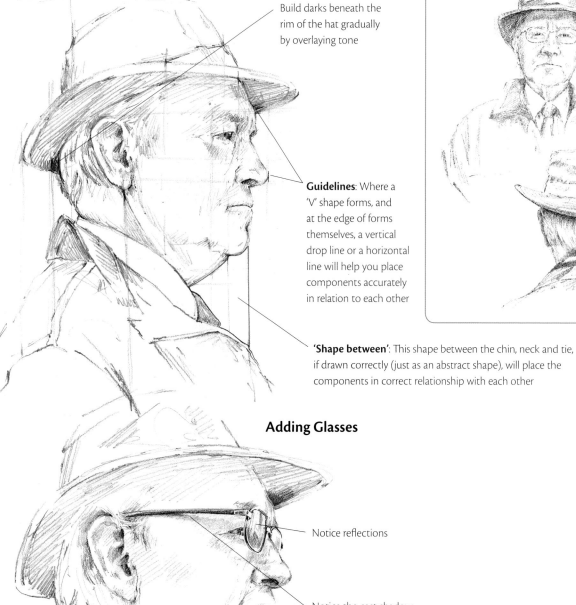

Build darks beneath the rim of the hat gradually by overlaying tone

Guidelines: Where a 'V' shape forms, and at the edge of forms themselves, a vertical drop line or a horizontal line will help you place components accurately in relation to each other

'Shape between': This shape between the chin, neck and tie, if drawn correctly (just as an abstract shape), will place the components in correct relationship with each other

Adding Glasses

Notice reflections

Notice the cast shadow that 'anchors' the glasses

Final Stage: Detailed Drawing

Now it is time to develop your final drawing.

MEDIA
- Faber-Castell: 3B
- Copier paper

1. Lost line at the top of the form

2. Look for opportunities to observe angles

3.

a) First directional strokes as underlay

b) Overlay tones to build intensity

c) Final dark overlay

When I draw hands how can I prevent them looking like a bunch of bananas?

MEDIA
• Soft pencil
• Sketchbook paper

 Be on the lookout for angles and avoid hard (wire-like) diagrammatic outlines. Instead use on/off pressure lines to define the edge of the form. Look at (and draw) the negative shapes between the digits rather than concentrating on the fingers and thumb as individual forms separately.

Looking for Angles

Be aware of angles like these, rather than initially depicting curves. Draw angles first then soften with a curve over these, where required, afterwards

Negative shape – by drawing this shape correctly you will be placing the thumb in correct relationship with the fingers

Gathering Ideas

When the model is at rest, with their arm relaxing and hand devoid of tension, you have an opportunity to use your sketchbook to gather images like these and to take your time over their execution.

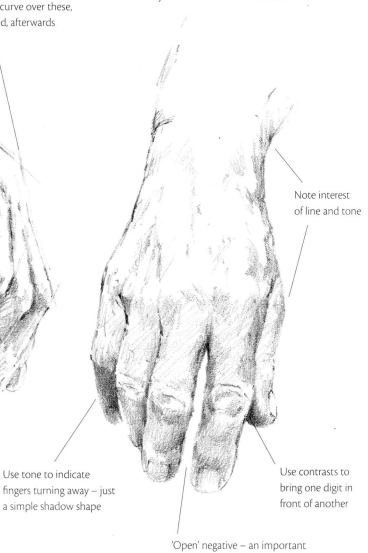

Note interest of line and tone

Use tone to indicate fingers turning away – just a simple shadow shape

Use contrasts to bring one digit in front of another

'Open' negative – an important 'shape between' that helps position the fingers on either side

Further Studies

Sketches like these rely on directional placing of tone, retention of untouched paper and erratically drawn lines to add interest to the interpretation.

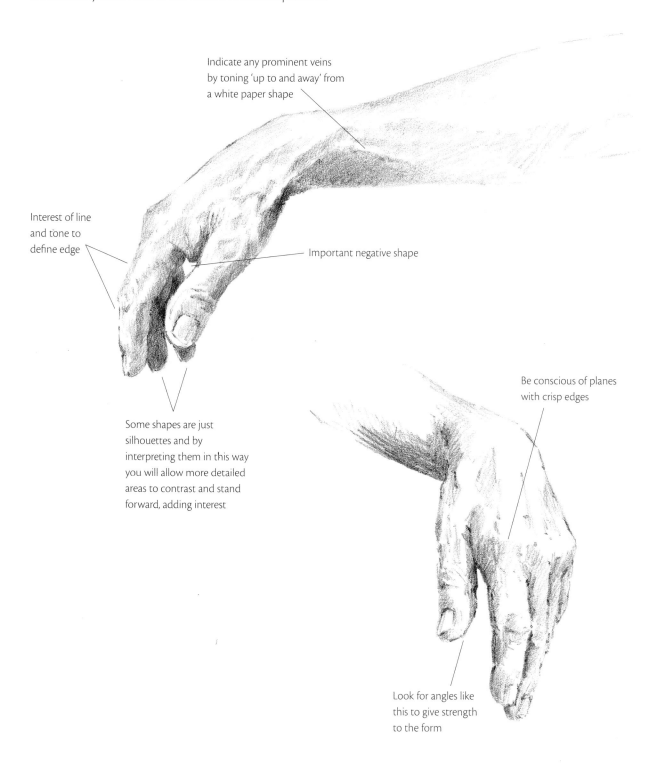

Indicate any prominent veins by toning 'up to and away' from a white paper shape

Interest of line and tone to define edge

Important negative shape

Some shapes are just silhouettes and by interpreting them in this way you will allow more detailed areas to contrast and stand forward, adding interest

Be conscious of planes with crisp edges

Look for angles like this to give strength to the form

Q **What techniques can I use to enhance the relationship between two figures?**

A This illustration of a mother and child, which includes strong shadow shapes, demonstrates how the techniques below can be used to enhance the relationship between the two figures.

On the opposite page, where the figures are closer together, the narrow negative space between them and the subtle shadows help to enhance their relationship to each other.

MEDIA
• Soft pencil
• Sketchbook paper

Mother and Child Study

Strong cast shadow shape

Minimum of shapes and lines on the mother's torso contrast with more use of line and tone on the child

Simple statement using strong contour lines

Maximum contrast for impact

TECHNIQUES: Shadow Lines and Shapes

1. Bags – Long and short zigzags indicate stress and weight

2. Clothing – Swiftly placed diagonal toning

3. Shadow shapes and lines – a) Grouping strokes, b) Twisting line, c) Zigzags

4. Crisp folds – Toning 'up to and away'

5. Cast shadows – Grazing application

6. Position forms – On/off pressure wandering lines

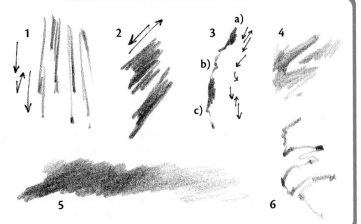

Negative and Shadow Shapes

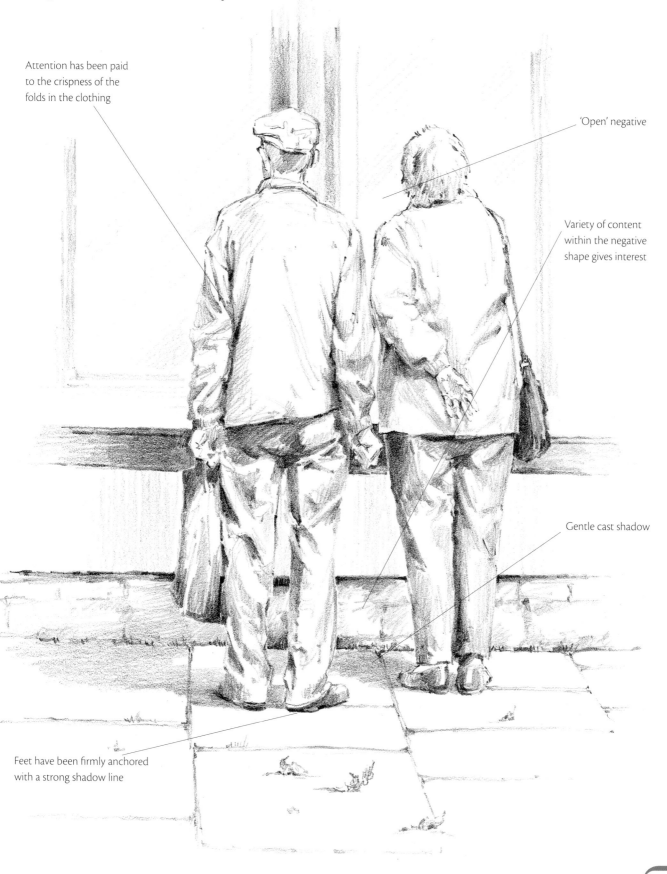

Attention has been paid to the crispness of the folds in the clothing

'Open' negative

Variety of content within the negative shape gives interest

Gentle cast shadow

Feet have been firmly anchored with a strong shadow line

What do you mean by the following terms in relation to figures: a) 'look for angles', b) 'follow the form', c) 'shadow shapes and shadow lines', d) 'relationships', and e) 'shapes between'?

 The best way to explain these terms is visually. To help you understand their meaning, I have pointed out where they are applicable in the following moving figure sketches.

> **MEDIA**
> • Faber-Castell: B
> • Bristol board

Look for Angles, Follow the Form and Shadow Shapes

Shadow lines of folds need to follow the direction of the form beneath

Look for angles in the folds

Shadow shape within the folds

Relationships and 'Shapes Between'

1. Large 'shape between':
a) Relationship of club to hair
b) Relationship of hair to shoulder
c) Relationship of top to trousers
d) Relationship of club head to figure's seat

2. Small 'shape between':
a) Underneath upper arm
b) Part of sleeve
c) Top of chest and front of body and the drop line used as a guide

3. Undulating edge line indicates the pull of fabric folds as a result of strong movement

4. These points were chosen as angles from which to draw helpful guidelines

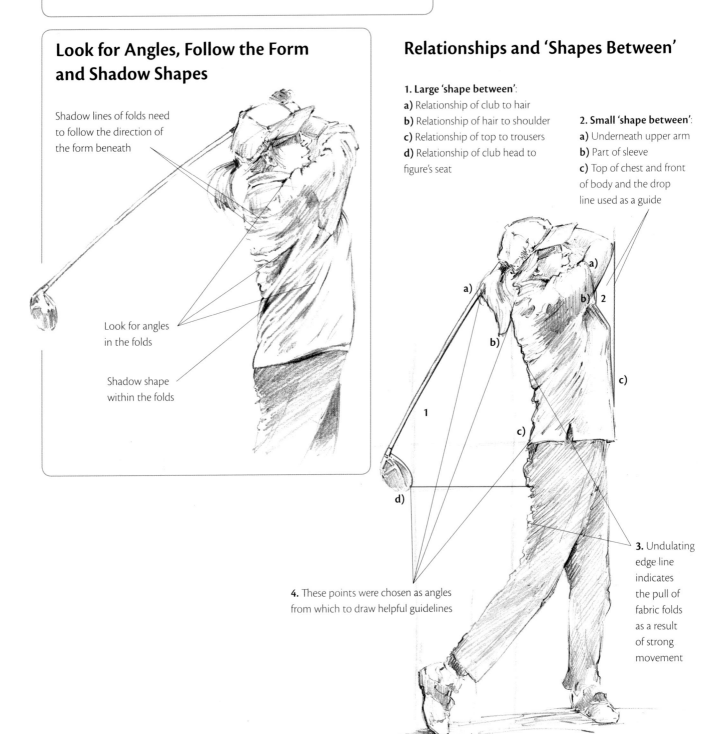

Focusing on Shapes

Often when drawing moving figures, such as the two examples below, it is important to forget the subject that you are drawing and instead simply look at the shapes to achieve more realistic results.

MEDIA
- Derwent Graphic: 3B
- Copier paper

Looking at Negative Shapes

Try not to think of how to draw a hand seen at this angle; just draw the shape you see

If you think primarily of the negative shapes and their relationship to each other, and draw these, you will find you have automatically placed the positive forms accurately in relation to each other

The impression of the far leg simply comprises a shadow shape

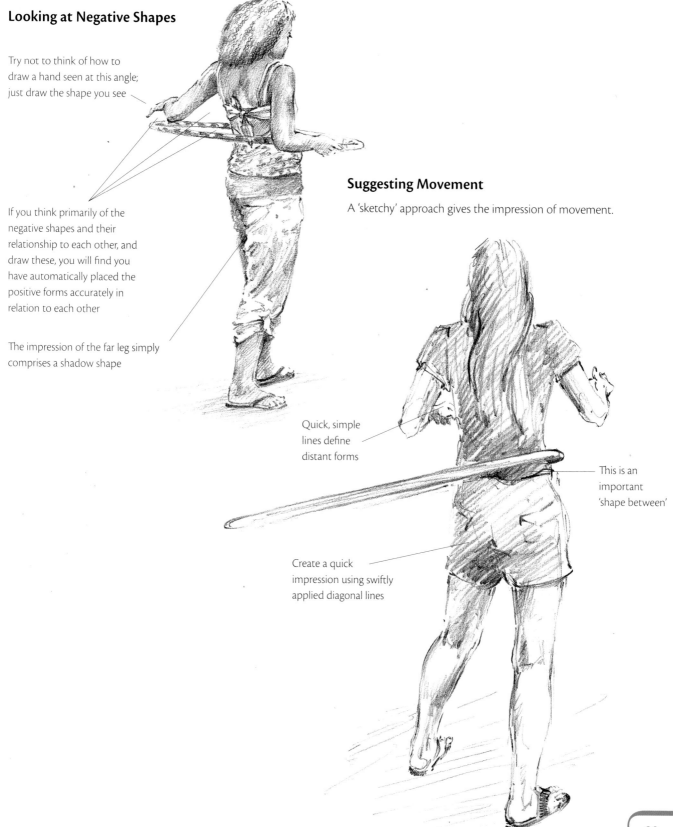

Suggesting Movement

A 'sketchy' approach gives the impression of movement.

Quick, simple lines define distant forms

This is an important 'shape between'

Create a quick impression using swiftly applied diagonal lines

Q **What is layout paper and what can I use it for?**

 A Layout paper is a very smooth, white, semi-transparent paper. You can use it for quick sketches to work out your compositions or exploratory drawings of individual images, making investigative sketches and playing with ideas.

MEDIA
• Derwent Graphic 6B
• Layout paper

Quick Sketches on Layout Paper

1. Guidelines are used to help establish the position of the rider in relation to the horse

2. b) Stronger lines confirm the position

2. a) First feint underdrawing

Using Layout Paper for Investigative Drawings

As layout paper is semi-transparent you can place your initial sketch up at a window (or on a light box) and, using another sheet of layout paper over the top, produce a stronger drawing. This will still keep your approach free to enhance or change certain areas.

The initial underdrawing can be seen before an adjustment to the leg position was made

Experimenting with Layout Paper

Contrasts in Relationships

There is fluidity between the horse and its rider that is not apparent when figures relate to machinery. Here, we have the contrast between the solidity of a bike and relationship of two figures with the machine.

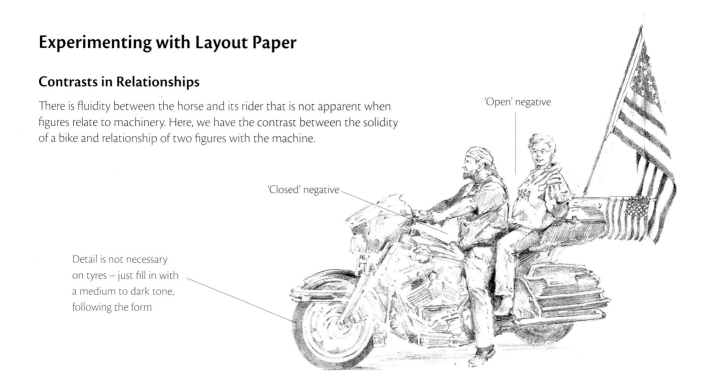

'Open' negative

'Closed' negative

Detail is not necessary on tyres – just fill in with a medium to dark tone, following the form

Moving Towards Abstraction

As on page 89, machinery also offers opportunities for abstract interpretations, by looking into reflections on chrome or the individual components of the engine. Layout paper is an ideal surface for experimentation.

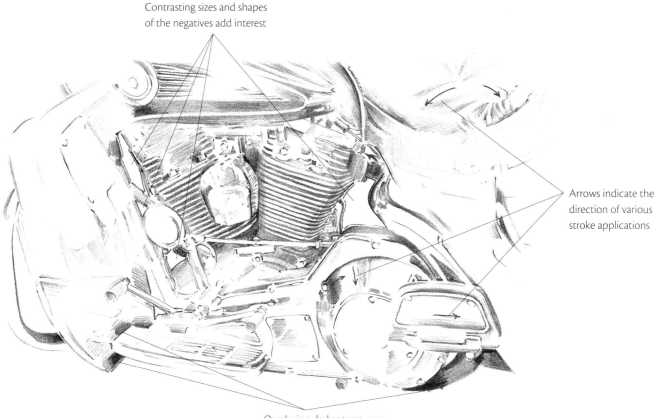

Contrasting sizes and shapes of the negatives add interest

Arrows indicate the direction of various stroke applications

Overlaying darker tone, over basic underdrawing, working 'up to and away' from light forms

Q When sketching figures from life, what stroke movements can I use for quick interpretations and, if figures remain still, for the addition of tonal shapes?

A The wandering line method of drawing, where the pencil remains in contact with the paper for most of the application, enables quick sketches to be made before the figures move.

MEDIA
- HB pencil (initial sketch)
- Soft pencil (main study)
- Copier paper

Wandering Lines that Find the Form

Most of these lines are a result of the pencil remaining in contact with the paper's surface during the execution of the drawing.

Curved lines follow the contours of more rounded forms

Lost line edge – where the pencil momentarily lifts from the paper's surface

Angular lines suggest crispness of clothing folds on the more angular forms

Applying Directional Tone

Directional toning can be applied using a soft pencil to enable tonal shapes to be placed rapidly.

Interesting on/off erratic pressure edge lines to avoid a 'wire-like' outline

Note the varied direction of stroke application relating to form

Faintly drawn vertical and horizontal guidelines help to anchor the figures to the ground convincingly with regard to weight distribution and balance

Shadows seen through negative shapes help relate the figures to the ground

Toning for Colour and Shadows

Overlaying tone to suggest body mass may take longer – however, if you use the white paper to indicate light colours and highlights, this will provide contrasts to create drama and reduce sketching time.

TIP If there is time to sketch the background in relation to the figures, it will help you understand scale and proportions regarding distance

Creating contrasts to bring light forms forward

Applying strokes directionally, having regard for form

Lost line included for interest, as a continuous edge line is unnecessary

Diagonal application for initial blocking in of tone

Overlaying tone to describe form

Q **Can you remind me of a few things to consider when drawing children?**

A From the eyes and the shape of their limbs, to their clothing, there are a number of aspects to consider when drawing children, which I will illustrate in the studies below and opposite.

MEDIA
- Derwent Graphic: 6B
- Saunders Waterford HP High White paper

TIP *If you intend to work from a photograph, try to capture a moment when the child is unaware of your intentions and so will not appear to be 'posed'*

Child at Play

A child's eyes, in relation to the face as a whole, appear larger than those of an adult

To indicate clothing in sunlight, place gentle toning behind the form

Negative shapes like this will help you achieve the correct proportions of a child's limbs in relation to their body

Tone directionally, 'up to and away' from the lighter form, gently indicating the cast shadow over soft skin

Natural Positions

It is important to think about the position and stance of the child or children that you are studying, to achieve a study that is as natural as possible.

MEDIA
- Derwent Onyx Dark
- Copier paper

Group Study

The bony framework of a young child's head, compared to that of an adult, is proportionately larger

Different personalities may be expressed in their body movements

Individual Studies

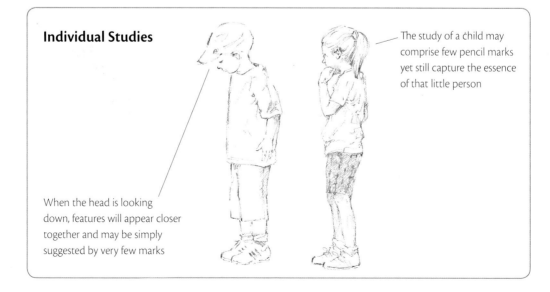

The study of a child may comprise few pencil marks yet still capture the essence of that little person

When the head is looking down, features will appear closer together and may be simply suggested by very few marks

Q How can I sketch active figures in an interesting arrangement in relation to each other and when seen as part of a street scene in relation to buildings?

A Look at the following studies for ideas on how to create interesting relationships between figures in a number of situations.

MEDIA

- Derwent Graphic: 6B
- Saunders Waterford HP High White paper

Looking at Figures in Relation to Each Other

The arrangement of overlapping areas of these two figures and their separation from the other two, provides interesting contrasts

Limbs overlapping slightly provide an interesting relationship

The bag, seen within a negative space, overlaps a central guideline providing more interest within the shape

The difference in these negative shapes adds interest

Street Scene: Initial Sketch

This quick sketch of figures in a street scene is my preliminary drawing for the sketch opposite.

MEDIA

- Derwent Graphic: B
- Layout paper

Street Scene: Final Study

The sketchy lines used to represent figures suggest activity and the arrangement of figures (with shadows) in relation to the contrasting textures of buildings and foliage, provides an interesting scene.

Distant figures are indicated with simple dark silhouette shapes

Pots and umbrellas provide contrasting static shapes against the activity of the figures

'S' shape arrangement takes the eye into the picture

Q What techniques should I use to illustrate different types of animal hair?

A In the techniques sections below and opposite, I have outlined the smooth toning techniques necessary for depicting a short-haired animal and the 'chiselling' method required for a woolly animal.

Short-Haired Animal: Bull

Leave untouched white paper to suggest raised muscles

Strong contrast of dark behind light form to bring it forward

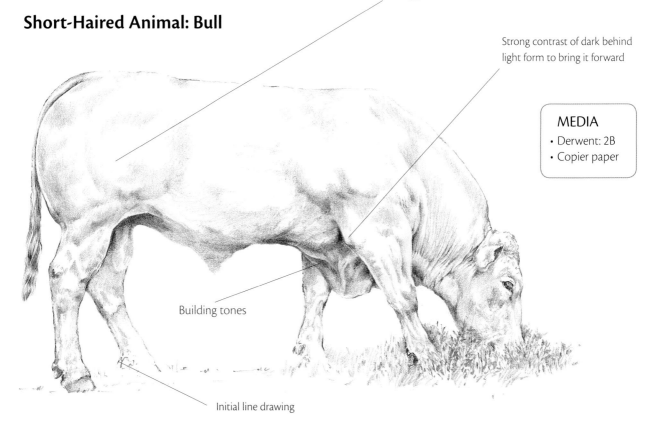

Building tones

Initial line drawing

MEDIA
- Derwent: 2B
- Copier paper

TECHNIQUES: Short Hair

When studying a short-haired animal, it is useful to practise smooth toning of abstract shapes:

1. Make a tonal block

2. Use the resulting fine side of the pencil strip to create a delicate erratic pressure line

3. Series of on/off pressure lines

4. Rich contrasts

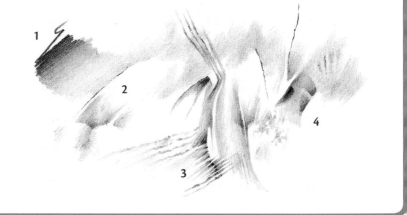

TECHNIQUES: Long Hair/Wool

When depicting a long-haired or woolly animal, such as the lamb below or the cow shown on page 3, focus on counterchange: dark tone against light followed by light against dark.

1. Establish a chisel side to your pencil strip for a wide line stroke

2. With varied pressure, move the pencil around unevenly with a dark tone

3. Add paler tones and leave some white paper for raised areas

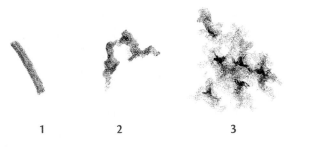

1 2 3

Woolly Animal: Lamb

Rich dark tone behind light form for maximum contrast

Building tonal overlays

Random application of tone

TIP *Hone your skills at subtle toning by practising purely abstract shapes and lines*

Vertical toning over diagonal

Diagonal toning

Form against background need not be clearly defined in some areas

Untouched paper depicts the lightest areas

Dark tone against light followed by light against dark – counterchange

MEDIA
- Faber-Castell: 5B
- Drawing cartridge paper

Q Can you demonstrate the differences between a line drawing, a line and tone sketch and a detailed drawing for the texture of feathers?

A The following studies of a chicken demonstrate the differences between these types of studies.

MEDIA
• Faber-Castell: 6B
• Copier paper

TIP *To add interest to your drawings try to avoid a hard, continuous dramatic outline. – use erratic on/off pressure on the pencil to produce far more effective lines*

Line Drawing

A line drawing may comprise the use of wandering lines that find the form by travelling around it. It may be an outlined illustration, representing the image in a rather flat interpretation or it may comprise a variety of directionally drawn lines, as shown below.

A line and tone drawing may comprise:
a) 'Wandering lines'
b) Outlines
c) A variety of directionally drawn lines

Line and Tone Sketch

In a line and tone sketch some lines, for example those around the bird's breast, describe the form by the direction in which they are applied, where others indicate feather shapes in a loose representation.

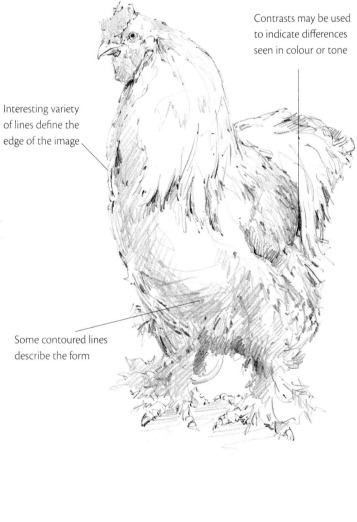

Contrasts may be used to indicate differences seen in colour or tone

Interesting variety of lines define the edge of the image

Some contoured lines describe the form

a)

b)

c)

Detail Study

The final study uses a variety of tones and shapes to create contrasts and form the feather shapes realistically.

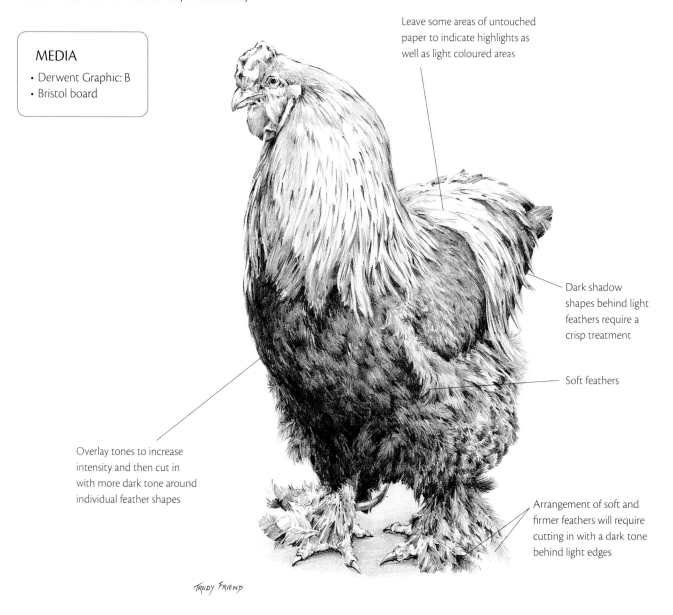

MEDIA
- Derwent Graphic: B
- Bristol board

Leave some areas of untouched paper to indicate highlights as well as light coloured areas

Dark shadow shapes behind light feathers require a crisp treatment

Soft feathers

Overlay tones to increase intensity and then cut in with more dark tone around individual feather shapes

Arrangement of soft and firmer feathers will require cutting in with a dark tone behind light edges

TRUDY FRIEND

TECHNIQUES: Feathers

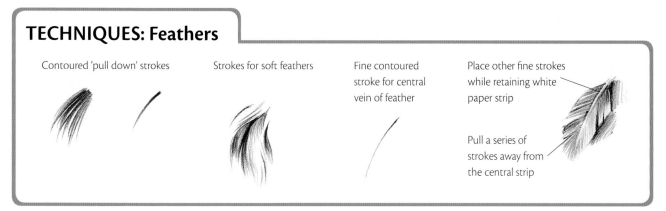

Contoured 'pull down' strokes

Strokes for soft feathers

Fine contoured stroke for central vein of feather

Place other fine strokes while retaining white paper strip

Pull a series of strokes away from the central strip

Q How can I achieve the effect of feather shape and pattern following the form of a bird?

A Analyse the shapes of the markings, as it is these that define the form. Start with a few preliminary sketches before your final study.

MEDIA
- Faber-Castell: 6B
- Copier paper

Preliminary Sketches

Counterchange: light against dark followed by dark against light will ensure the form takes shape

Placing the suggestion of a background will help you bring the light form of the bird forward

Crisp light edges against a dark behind will accentuate contrasts that enhance form

Notice how the feathers appear foreshortened when the head is turned in this position (see opposite)

Final Study

8. Practise executing the marks in the positions you see them: avoid placing them uniformly or at random without consideration for the form over which they pass

7. These marks comprise on/off pressure strokes in order to widen in the centre and taper at the ends

6. Gently graze tone to suggest shadow

5. Note curves and undulations

1. Marks like these consist of a number of sweeping strokes applied using a sharp pencil

2. Work down, around the shape, and up the other side as an exercise in stroke direction for feathers

3. It is important to place the first stroke in the correct direction for the others to follow

4. Gently tone up to the central area before adding the final on/off pressure contoured sweeping stroke for the centre vein

Wood Duck

This small study of a wood duck demonstrates a variety of other markings on a different species of bird.

Q **How can I achieve the impression of a wire fence in front of an image of an animal?**

A Use counterchange, where the wire appears dark when it passes in front of light parts of the form yet light when seen in front of dark areas of the animal, to achieve the desired effect.

MEDIA
- Koh-I-Noor Progresso: 8B
- Sketchbook paper

Lost line edge – light against light

First sketch loosely places the image before tonal overlays build the drawing

Techniques: Counterchange

1. Firm pressure   **2.** Lift pressure

3. Twist the pencil and work into an on/off pressure line

4. The twisting on/off pressure line positions dark wire

5. With zigzag grazing movements, work 'up to and away' from a light strip that is a continuation of the dark

TIP *Graze the background tone ('up to and away' from light edges) with light pressure first to establish positions, then overlay as necessary to increase the intensity of tone*

Tone 'up to and away' from light wire using light pressure for pale underdrawing initially to establish positions

Build layers of tone on each other to increase density of shadows and markings on the pig

Demonstration of How Lost Lines Occur

1. Lost line edges

2. Tonal mark

3. Varied tones

TIP *Use artist's licence and notice where a simple mark is all that is necessary to indicate the subject, rather than trying to include every detail you see*

Q **How can I achieve the effect that can be seen when light behind a form creates the impression of a halo of light animal hair/fur against a darker background?**

A There are a number of delicate stages to work through, which are explained in detail on the opposite page.

Achieving the 'Halo' Effect

The halo effect

Cut in with a dark tone behind the form to establish a light edge

Counterchange: light against dark followed by dark against light

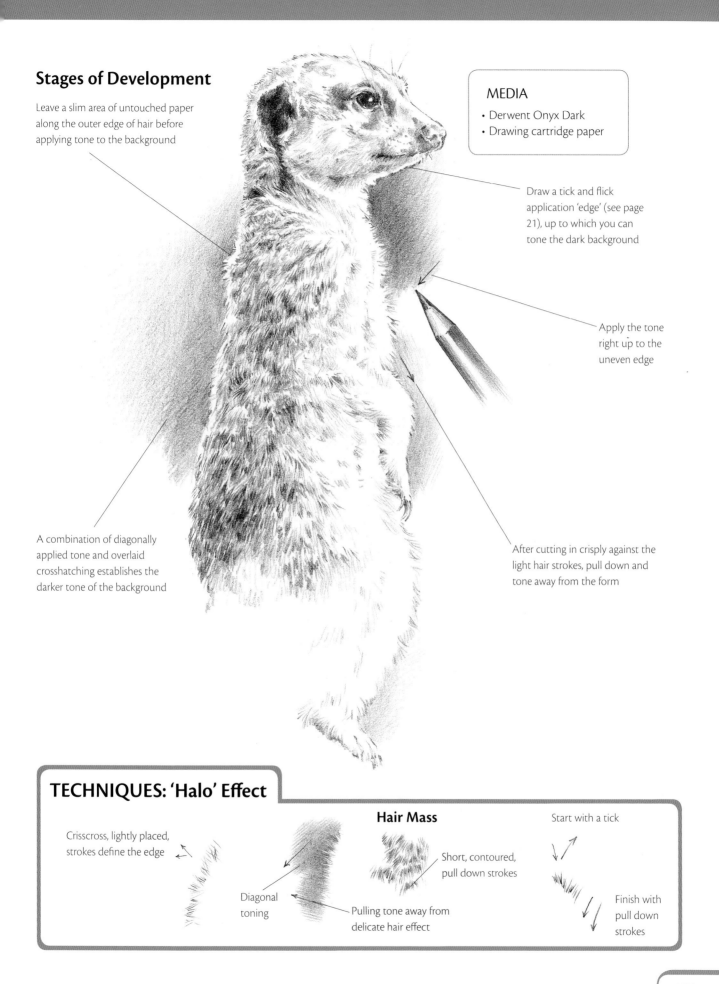

Stages of Development

Leave a slim area of untouched paper along the outer edge of hair before applying tone to the background

MEDIA
• Derwent Onyx Dark
• Drawing cartridge paper

Draw a tick and flick application 'edge' (see page 21), up to which you can tone the dark background

Apply the tone right up to the uneven edge

A combination of diagonally applied tone and overlaid crosshatching establishes the darker tone of the background

After cutting in crisply against the light hair strokes, pull down and tone away from the form

TECHNIQUES: 'Halo' Effect

Crisscross, lightly placed, strokes define the edge

Hair Mass

Start with a tick

Short, contoured, pull down strokes

Diagonal toning

Pulling tone away from delicate hair effect

Finish with pull down strokes

Q **What pencil stroke techniques can you suggest for depicting movement?**

A Swift, varied pressure strokes that follow the form and the direction of movement are important for the initial drawing, as demonstrated in the far goat below.

MEDIA
- Derwent Onyx Dark
- Bristol board

TIP *Dark graphite pencil delivers rich, jet-black tones and is ideal for quick, expressive sketches as well as detailed work*

Goats at Play

Although fine detail has been used for this drawing, the positions themselves, with the inclusion of interesting negative shapes between the two forms, accentuate the impression of movement. Make use of strong tonal contrasts which encourage the viewer's eye to move through the drawing.

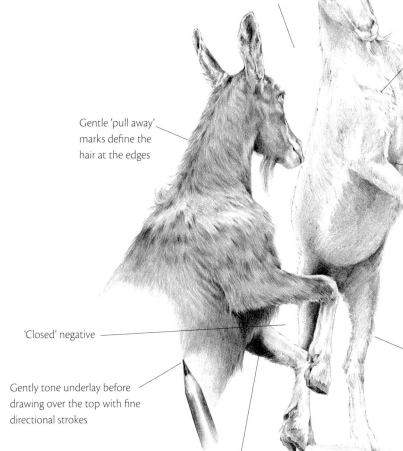

a) Lightly draw the shape of the eye, observing the angle at which it is seen

b) Add a dark pupil and leave a small highlight

'Open' negative

Indicate the direction of hair growth

Gentle 'pull away' marks define the hair at the edges

Tone 'up to and away' from the light form to bring it forward

Fine line is executed 'on your toes'

'Closed' negative

Gently tone underlay before drawing over the top with fine directional strokes

This study shows the basic underdrawing before tonal overlays are applied (as shown in the dark goat representation)

With onyx you can achieve rich darks – build these gradually by overlaying tone

Bird in Flight

Strong, bold strokes applied using a loose style are effective for depicting movement. In this study where wing movement is the main focus, sweeping strokes combined with the zigzag application depicts length of feathers and pattern, respectively.

MEDIA
- Derwent Graphitone: 8B
- Sketchbook paper

Cast shadow shape is overlaid on the initial drawing, after which darks are enhanced

Closed zigzag application of tone creates pattern

Shadow shapes

Darkest dark behind lightest light form for maximum contrast

Feather seen as a silhouette

Negative shape

TECHNIQUES: Fur and Feathers

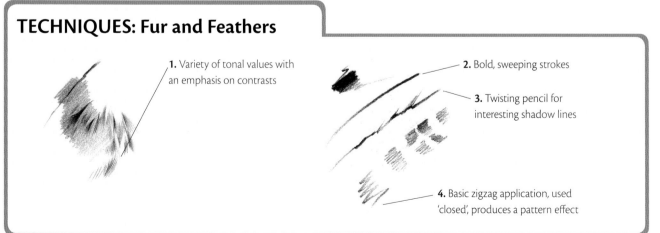

1. Variety of tonal values with an emphasis on contrasts

2. Bold, sweeping strokes

3. Twisting pencil for interesting shadow lines

4. Basic zigzag application, used 'closed', produces a pattern effect

Q Can you suggest which pencils and papers could work well together for detail studies in looser and tighter interpretations?

 A When you have more time to look into and depict detail (as shown below), harder pencil grades, for example HB, B and 2B, will work well on a smooth white surface like Bristol board. For a looser, more sketchy approach drawing cartridge paper works well with softer grades, for example, 3B, 4B and 5B, when the images are relatively small. For larger, looser interpretations you could try graphite sticks or blocks on sketchbook paper (see the bird study drawn in graphite stick on page 119).

Hoof Studies in Harder Grade Pencils

These studies are drawn on Bristol board using hard-grade pencils, e.g. HB, B and 2B.

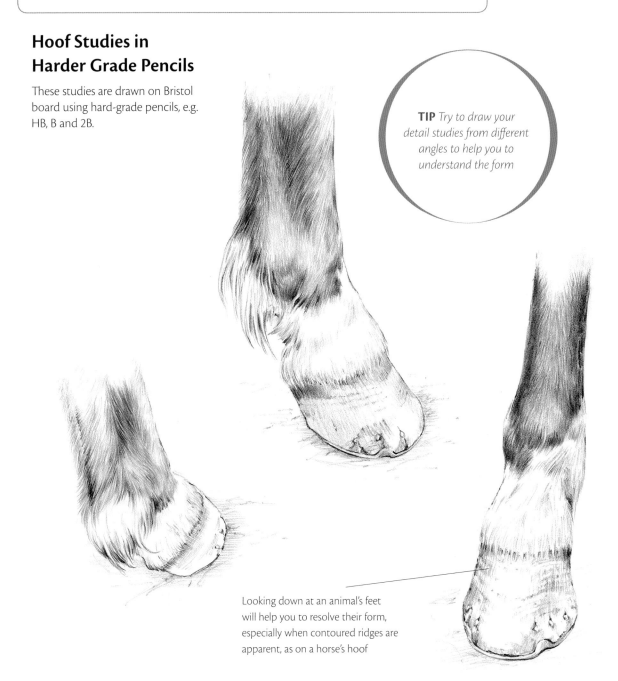

TIP *Try to draw your detail studies from different angles to help you to understand the form*

Looking down at an animal's feet will help you to resolve their form, especially when contoured ridges are apparent, as on a horse's hoof

Rhino Studies in Soft Pencil

Softer pencils have been used for the studies on this page. A 5B is ideal for detailed studies like this. Detail studies can help you understand your subject more, as they give you time to examine certain areas in greater depth. Sketching from life in a zoo will help you develop your observational skills.

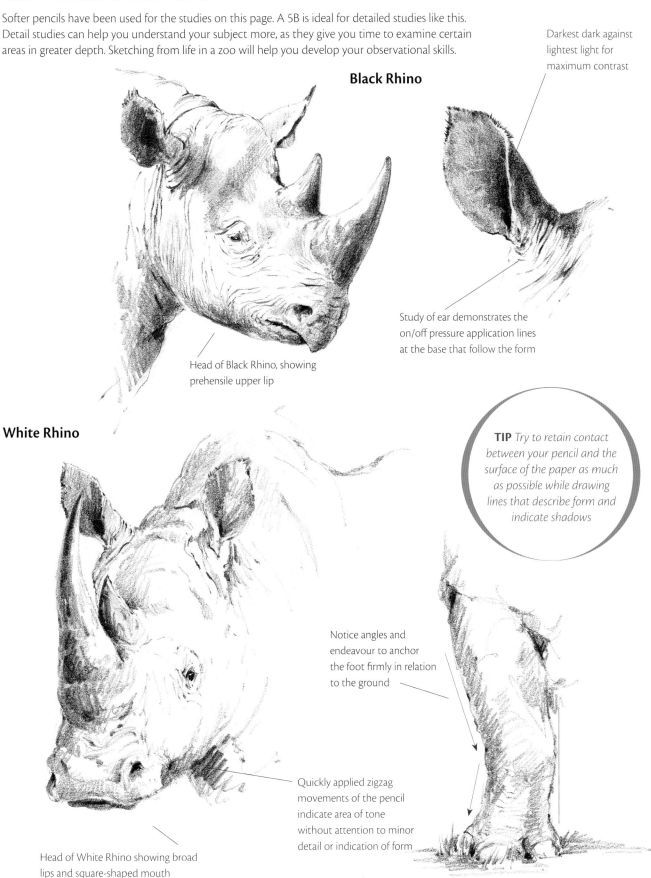

Black Rhino

Darkest dark against lightest light for maximum contrast

Study of ear demonstrates the on/off pressure application lines at the base that follow the form

Head of Black Rhino, showing prehensile upper lip

White Rhino

TIP *Try to retain contact between your pencil and the surface of the paper as much as possible while drawing lines that describe form and indicate shadows*

Notice angles and endeavour to anchor the foot firmly in relation to the ground

Quickly applied zigzag movements of the pencil indicate area of tone without attention to minor detail or indication of form

Head of White Rhino showing broad lips and square-shaped mouth

Q **Can you explain how to use a water-soluble pencil for black fur or hair?**

A The effects you are able to achieve will often depend on the surface of the paper on which you have chosen to work. This image is executed on Bristol board, which is a smooth surface. Gently brushing clear water across the drawn image will immediately create the effect of cast shadows.

Zebra Study

TIP Use a fine brush with a good point for delicate work

First stage: Blocking in to indicate position of markings

Second stage: Overlaying darker tone

Third stage: Depicting uneven edges using tick and flick and pull down movements to indicate light hairs crossing into dark bands/stripes or dark hairs over light areas

Fourth stage: Gentle wet brush movements that indicate shadow areas by blending the graphite

TECHNIQUES: Zebra

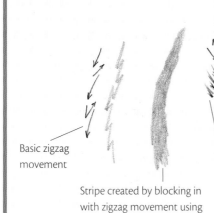

Basic zigzag movement

Stripe created by blocking in with zigzag movement using the chisel side of the pencil

Downward movement and upward flick

Pull down movements

Pull down movements create effect of dark hair over white

Tick and flick to create white hairs over dark

When stripe has been overlaid with tone to create intensity, a swift wash of clean water over the graphite will give the impression of cast shadow

The edge of the stripe may be softened with short pull down movements – working 'on your toes' (with the tip of the brush held vertically)

122

Q Can you suggest paper and pencils that work well together for a drawing of a predominantly black dog that has coloured points?

A This demonstration shows the effect of a dark wash (8B) Derwent sketching pencil on lightweight Bockingford paper. Derwent's range of lightly tinted water-soluble graphite pencils, Graphitint, are ideal for your requirements. The subtle shades produced when they are used dry alter dramatically when water is added, resulting in vibrant hues.

Dog Study

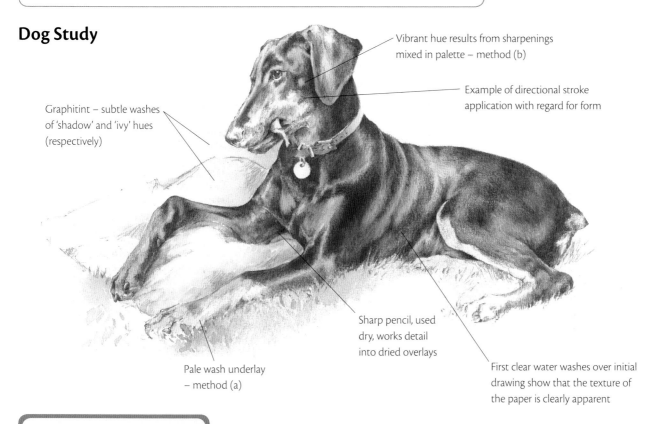

Vibrant hue results from sharpenings mixed in palette – method (b)

Example of directional stroke application with regard for form

Graphitint – subtle washes of 'shadow' and 'ivy' hues (respectively)

Sharp pencil, used dry, works detail into dried overlays

Pale wash underlay – method (a)

First clear water washes over initial drawing show that the texture of the paper is clearly apparent

TECHNIQUES: Dog

Note that the use of fixative on a drawing where you have worked with Graphitint may cause the effects produced to change. It is advisable to experiment with examples first.

1. **a)** Chestnut dry on dry

Water added

b) Chestnut sharpenings in palette well with water added

Note the difference in hue that can result from these two methods of mixing with water

2. c) Taking pigment from the pencil strip using a wet brush in order to paint directionally on to the paper's surface

3. Other tints (colours) used:

a) Shadow: tint on cushion

b) Ivy: grass

c) Green Grey: grass

4. Derwent sketching water-soluble graphite dark wash 8B dry on the textured Bockingford surface

Dark wash

5. Water added

MEDIA
- Derwent Graphic: soft watercolour pencil
- Drawing cartridge paper

Q **Will you show how the eight basic stroke movements (see pages 18–21) may be translated into watercolour brushwork?**

A Yes, most applications translate easily for use with the brush. Remaining with the animal theme, I have demonstrated a transition in this illustration to clearly depict similarities between pencil strokes and brushstrokes. There is only one obvious difference, which is with the grazing application, where water brushwork is used in the form of a wash.

Basic Stroke Applications

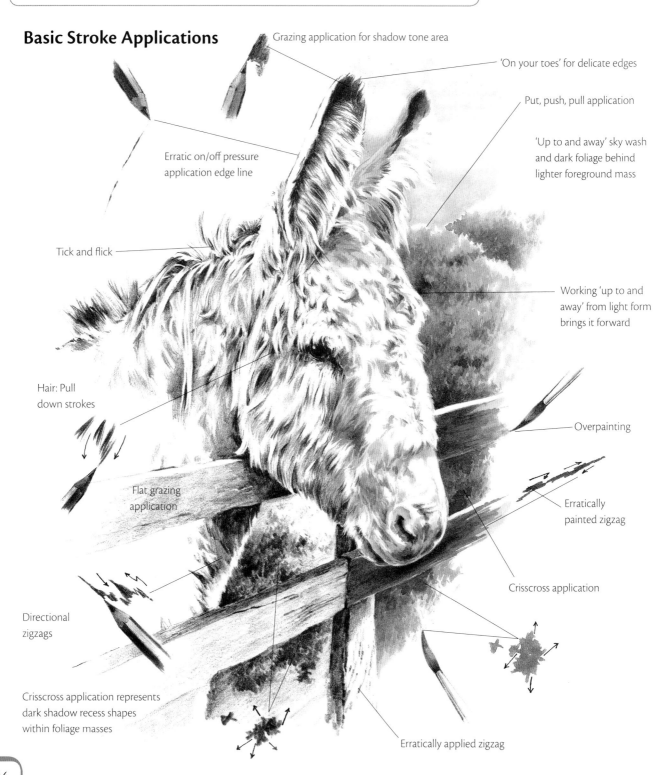

Grazing application for shadow tone area

'On your toes' for delicate edges

Put, push, pull application

'Up to and away' sky wash and dark foliage behind lighter foreground mass

Erratic on/off pressure application edge line

Tick and flick

Working 'up to and away' from light form brings it forward

Hair: Pull down strokes

Overpainting

Flat grazing application

Erratically painted zigzag

Crisscross application

Directional zigzags

Crisscross application represents dark shadow recess shapes within foliage masses

Erratically applied zigzag

From Pencil into Brushstroke

On the opposite page, I have demonstrated how some of the eight basic stroke movements in pencil can translate to watercolour, in order for you to make comparisons in technique. Below are examples to demonstrate how you can use the eight basic stroke movements for brushwork as well as pencil application, as the movements and pressure variations are the same. However, the inclusion of water combined with the soft hairs of a brush will create different effects in some instances.

1. On/Off Pressure Stroke

Note how the width achieved by pressure on a brush will, depending on the size of the brush, be wider when pressure is placed than those produced by a soft pencil

2. Erratic Pressure Stroke

a) Erratically applied stroke movements appear very similar to those achieved with a pencil

b) Twist strokes of the pencil are substituted by short angular movements when using a brush

c) Zigzag movements appear the same when achieved with a brush as with the pencil

3. Grazing Application

Grazing with a pencil is the same as applying a wash in watercolour

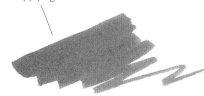

4. Put, Push, Pull Application

a) Putting a loaded brush on the paper's surface and pushing upwards (directionally) is an ideal method of representing massed foliage (see opposite)

b) Pull down strokes are useful for hair and grass representations

5. 'On Your Toes' Application

Using the very tip of a pointed brush held vertically to the paper's surface will achieve the most delicate of marks

6. Crisscross Movement

These movements, with the brush almost in constant contact with the paper's surface, produce instant massed arrangement of strokes

Crisscross movements applied 'on your toes' as individual strokes

7. 'Up to and Away' Movement

Working 'up to and away' from a light image will make it stand forward

Work up to

Work away from

8. Tick and Flick Movement

When your ticks end as flat shapes add pull down strokes to them before the paint dries to taper the tips

Glossary

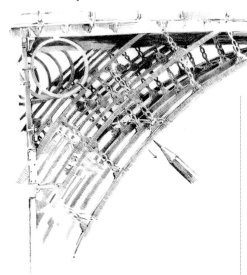

Iron bridge structure

Chisel edge of the pencil: The wider edge of the pencil, used for applying cast shadow areas and shadows when toning.

Constant contact: Maintaining contact as you draw to retain continuity and 'flow'.

Contrasts: Achieve maximum contrast by placing the darkest of your dark tones directly against the untouched white paper.

Crisscross stroke application: The varied directional movements involved in placing the strokes, to create interest of texture.

Crosshatching: Placing strokes in one direction then overlapping in the opposite direction, to create a solid tonal mass or, if slightly apart, an 'open weave' effect.

Describing form: Follow the form of the object you are depicting by imagining a tiny insect walking over the surface of the object and let your pencil follow the direction the insect would take.

Direction: This may refer to the direction in which an artist encourages the viewer's eye to travel through a composition or to the direction in which your pencil strokes are applied to the paper.

Edit in or out: Choosing to include or omit certain components within a composition.

Erratic pressure strokes: Pressing on and lifting from the paper unevenly to achieve interest of texture.

Fixative: Spraying with a fixative product will prevent drawings from smudging.

Grazing: Letting your pencil 'graze' across the paper's surface to create tone.

Guidelines: Vertically or horizontally drawn lines (of varied length) that relate an area or component to another, some distance away, in a composition.

Highlights: Pencil techniques rely on the retention of white paper for the depiction of highlighted areas.

Investigative sketch: Initial sketch or drawing through which we inquire into and examine in detail the subject we have chosen to depict to decide what needs to be edited in or out.

Lost lines: When the background (or adjacent image) tone is very similar, causing the two to appear to merge in places, to add interest and a sense of reality to your pictures.

Monochrome: A drawing that is a single-colour representation, relying on tonal values for contrasts.

Negative shapes: These may be dark or light. Dark negatives are shadowed recessive shapes, for example, where an animal or object may disappear into the shape. The shapes between foliage masses between which birds may fly to the sky beyond are light negatives.

On/off pressure: By applying and then lifting pressure on a pencil, interest of line/shape may be achieved.

'On your toes': Small dots, dashes, lines and grazing are achieved by using the tip of the pencil or brush, which is held vertical to the paper's surface.

One stroke images: Using a single brush stroke or soft graphite stroke to produce a recognizable shape.

Put, push, pull: Directing the stroke movement in relation to your subject.

Reflected light: On a spherical or cylindrical shape, leave a light edge on the dark (shadow) side before it meets its dark cast shadow.
This depicts light that is reflected back on to the object's shadow side from the light of its support.

Relationships: Relating one form to another with the help of guidelines.

Texture: Creating character of surface using textured paper or creating texture with your pencil marks.

Tick and flick: Using the pencil to make tick movements to create grasses and hair.

Twists and turns: By twisting the pencil between your fingers you will be able to create interest of line.

Underdrawing: The initial drawing in line/tone on which other tones can be overlaid.

'Up to and away': Cut in crisply up to the image to be defined, before taking the tone away from the form.

Wandering lines: Constant contact with the paper's surface throughout the application of a line that wanders around the form.

Suppliers

UK

Derwent
The Cumberland Pencil Company
Derwent House
Jubilee Road
Lillyhall Business Park
Workington
Cumbria CA14 4HS
Tel: 01900 609599
www.pencils.co.uk
For high-quality drawing materials

Inveresk
St Cuthbert's Mill
Wells
Somerset BA5 1AG
Tel: 01749 672015
www.inveresk.co.uk
*For Saunders Waterford and
Bockingford papers*

SAA (Society for All Artists)
PO BOX 50
Newark
Nottinghamshire NG23 5GY
Tel (UK sales): 0800 980 1123
Tel (non-UK sales): 01949 844050
www.saa.co.uk
For art supplies and sundries

Winsor & Newton
Whitefriars Avenue
Harrow
Middlesex HA3 5RH
Tel: 020 8424 3200
www.winsornewton.com
For papers and painting media

USA

Art Media
902 SW Yamhill
Portland
Oregon 97205
www.artmediaonline.com
For paper and other art media

Jerry's Artarama
Order Dept.
PO Box 58638J
Raleigh
North Carolina 27658-8638
Tel: 1-800-827-8478
www.jerrysartarama.com
For pencils, paper and other media

Madison Art Shop
17 Engleberg Terrace
Lakewood
New Jersey 08701
Tel: 1-800-961-1570
www.madisonartshop.com
For drawing and painting supplies

Europe

Faber-Castell
Vertrieb GmbH
Nürnberger Strasse 2
90546 Stein
Germany
Tel: +49 (0) 911 9965 0
www.faber-castell.com
For Pitt Artist pens

Koh-I-Noor Hardtmuth
F.A. Gerstnera 21/3
CZ 371 30 České Budějovice
Czech Republic
Tel: +420 389 000 200
www.koh-i-noor.eu
For pencils and other art media

Acknowledgments

Thank you to all friends and acquaintances who have provided some of the photographic reference material, without which I could not have produced such a variety of subject matter.

I would also like to thank my husband for his forbearance when, time after time, I had to refrain from being in his company, with the reason ... 'I have to work on my book'.

Sketch of dogs at play